THE DRURY

SPRING 20/20

True Stories

DANCING with SATAN

Mary Ann Cincinnati

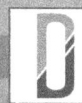
www.druryspublishing.com

— SPRING 20/20 —

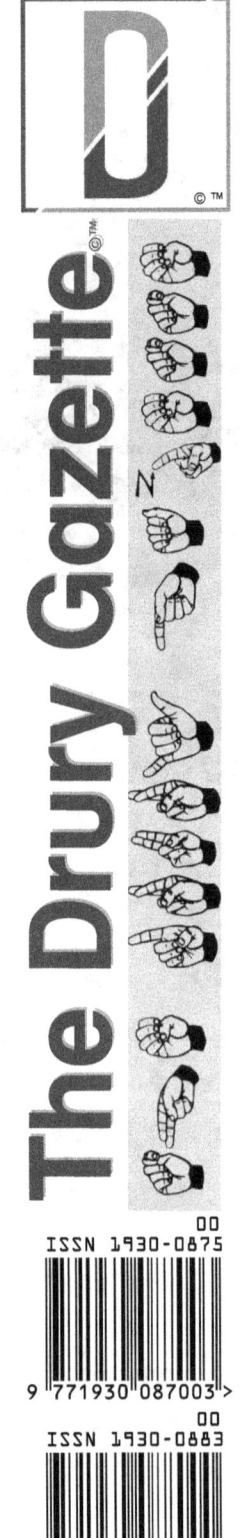

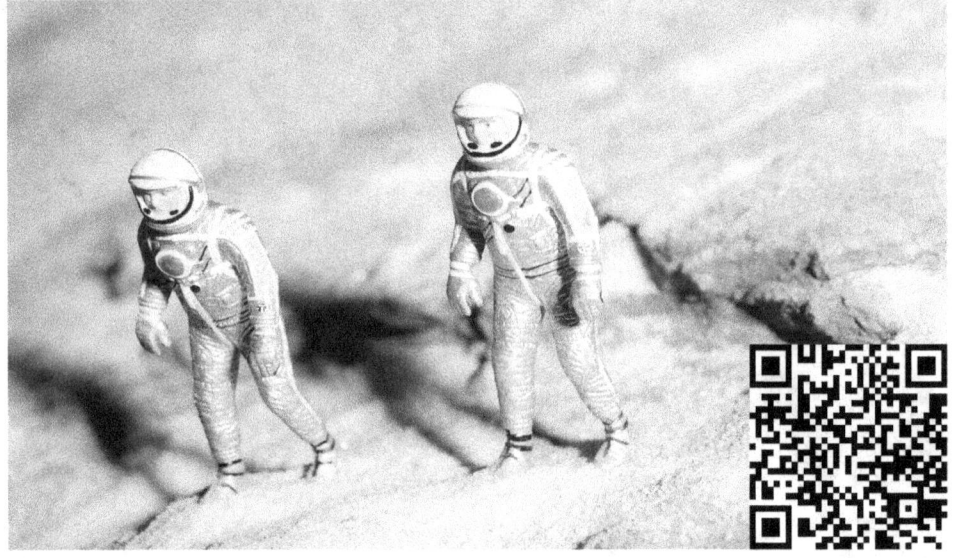

Staff
Gary Drury, Author / Editor / Journalist / Minister / Publisher

© 2020 by Gary Drury / Drury Gazette

All rights reserved. No part of this publication may be reproduced or transmitted in whole or in part in any form or by any means, electronic or mechanical, including photocopy, recording, or any information storage and retrieval system, known or unknown, without permission in writing from the publisher, except by a reviewer who may quote brief passages in a review to be printed in a newspaper, magazine or journal.

I reserve the exclusive right to edit, accept or reject any submission for any reason whatsoever without verbal or written notice. The author bears sole responsibility for his/her own work. The expression within this publication reflects the beliefs and philosophies of their originators and are not necessarily views and opinions of Gary Drury Publishing Ministries or The Drury Gazette.

Contact Information: No Phone Calls Accepted without prior appointment. For expedited correspondence please visit www.druryspublishing.com.

Serious inquiries ONLY, please. Spammers will be reported to their ISPs, authorities and legal action may ensue.

The Drury Gazette promotes raising authors. Its a non-profit private corporation sole ministry encourages strong Christian values, defends and supports inalienable rights, The Republic-United States of America Constitution: freedoms of press, religion & speech, etc. ***26 U.S. Code § 508 (c) (1) (A).** Gifts are tax deductible.

The Drury Gazette Digital is provided free of charge. Please adhere to any ©, ™, and SM mark laws. Nonetheless, this PDF must remain whole perpetually. No alterations permitted. Also, we encouraged you to share, however, not to sell, lease, rent or monetize the PDFs in any way whatsoever.

Permission is granted you to print out a copy for your own personal use. Absolutely, no authorization deduced for mass printed dissemination. The authorization is granted for email broadcasting provided no spamming and you are authorized to email such parties. Likewise, share with others to help spread God's word and authors gain recognition.

You can direct individuals interested in The Drury Gazette to www.druryspublishing.com to download a FREE issue. Enjoy!

SPRING 2020

ISBN-13: 9781660105243

ISSN: 1930-0875 (Print)
ISSN: 1930-0883 (PDF)

Gary Drury, Editor/Publisher. Established in 1982, Promotes well-grounded moral and spiritual values of all beliefs and faiths. I am devoted to creative expression and free speech. Correspondence, submissions, supportive donations and subscriptions should be directed to the publisher. — Your Success Is My Success © SM —

The Drury Gazette © ™
by Gary Drury Publishing Ministries © ™

www.druryspublishing.com © ™

NON-PROFIT QUARTERLY PUBLICATION
508 (c) (1) (A)

Cover photo, design, and layout by Gary Drury © ™

Printed in The Republic-United States of America.

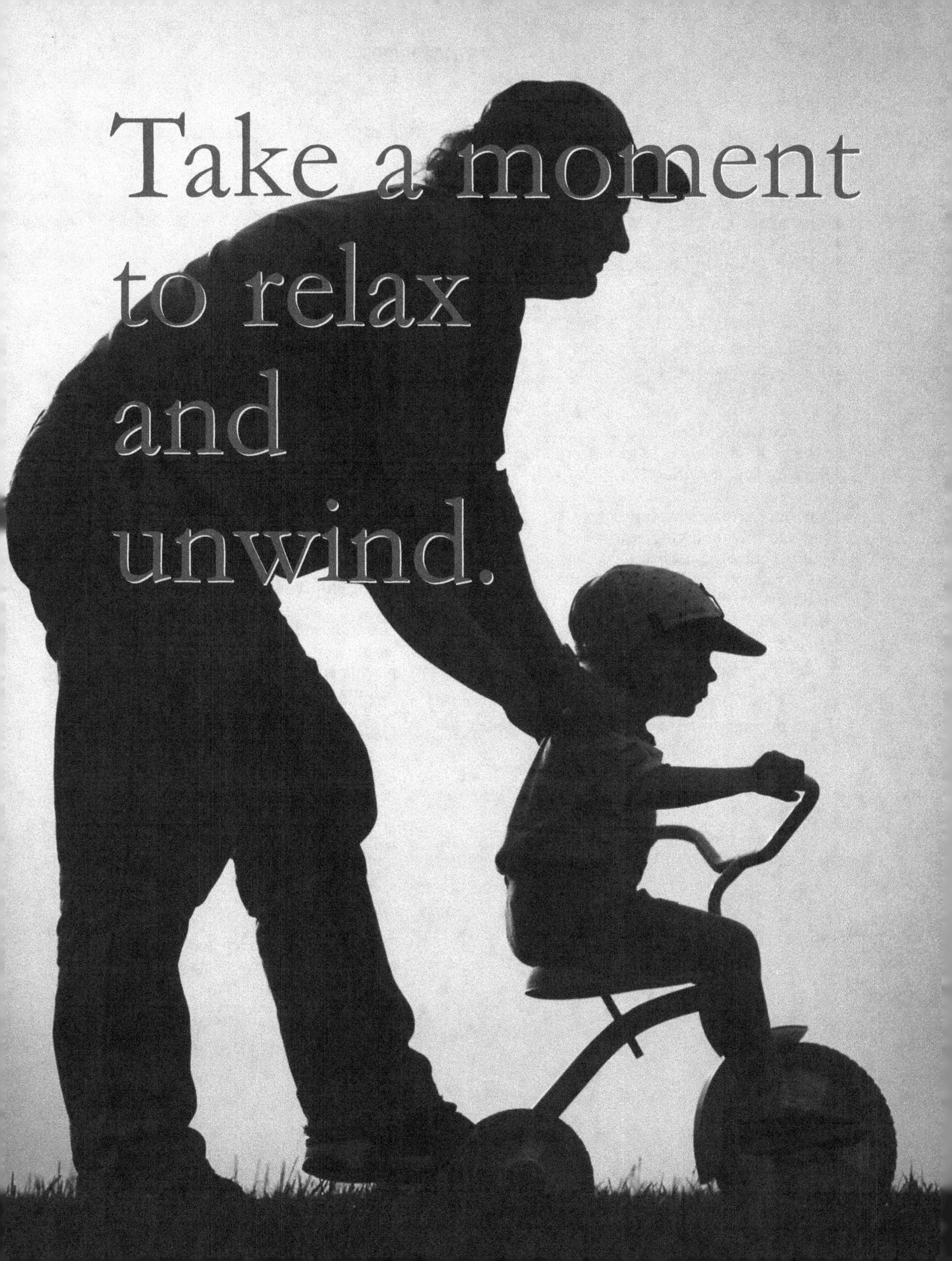
Take a moment
to relax
and
unwind.

Burning Heat

The temperatures rising
I'm so agonizingly hot
In this burning heat
I walked a thousand miles
To the ocean blue waters
seeking its cooling calm
releasing my burden
releasing my soul
releasing my heavy woes
Of burning Heat

How you cannot forgive,
Leave without a single word
Like a mirage or illusion
You are gone from my life
As if once you were never there
How vacant your loving heart
Your tongue of endless lies
Soulless before the Heaven's
Your devilish charms betray
Only a shadow of you remain there
In the black holes of my crying heart
How I feel the Burning Heat.

I realize now the service you did for me
When my pain rushes away maybe I will see
I am far better off without thee
Until that moment that time, I'm on knees
Drowning in plethora tears of the manmade sea
Locking my whaling heart, tossing the key

— © Gary A Drury

Keeping Busy

He surrounds himself with activities
keeping busy so he doesn't think,
not willing to ponder his loneliness
or the empty feeling in his heart.

His computer is his best friend
letting him escape into its screen
playing games for countless hours
helping him block out the lonely life he lives.

Deep in his heart, he wants to be loved
and when all is quiet
he sometimes thinks of how his life would be
if he could finally meet his one true love.

But deep down he believes
that being loved is an empty dream,
and that he is fated to be alone
to struggle through his life of misery.

To cope with his deep-felt pain
he tries not to think about his plight,
but feelings of loneliness still invade for
the need to be loved is stronger than any man.

— © Sheila B. Roark

Walking With

When I was nearly three, or so,
My mother used to let me go
Off through the woods, so I could play
With some cousins for the day.
It was a long walk for me
But I would always look to see
A pack of wolves who walked the trail
And they appeared there without fail!
I thought they were big dogs, you see,
Who came to keep me company?
I never felt the slightest fear
Just glad to see them walking near.
I talked to them, though I recall
Nothing of what I said at all.
Finally told my dad and him
Was much alarmed, that I could see,
His next trip home he brought a pet.
A big old dog. I can't forget
How thrilled I was. Rex was his name
And things were never quite the same.
He went with me just everywhere,
But wolves still followed so to share
Whatever Rex and I would do.
They just approved his presence too.
I later found out that his mother
Was a wolf so he was brother
To this pack that walked with me,
And they enjoyed his company.
For two more years, we were together
Friends, enjoying all the good weather.
We moved away back to the city
And it always seems a pity
That person couldn't know, like me,
The pleasure of the wolf company!

— © Betty L Hebert

Limping Duck

"Wind beneath my wings
to make me fly like an eagle"
so the song says,
family members are the
wind beneath my wings.
"Where your treasure is
there will your heart be also"
says the Sermon on The Mount.
Family members are my treasures.
That's all changed now,
they are all gone,
"Gone With The Wind!"
All just memories to fill
a heart and soul album.
People put flowers on graves
then depart and forget,
I prefer flowers in my heart
letting the memory set in cement!
I'm just a limping duck
who had run amuck;
Lord help me to get
off the ground and be
bound for heaven's glory!

— © Gerald Heyder

The Memory of the past Get Warm Most of Us

The memory of the past warm most of us,
Our tired hearts are still knocking,
But everyone feels the beginning of the end,
To which we stubbornly sail.
Through the sharp thresholds of being
Carries us along rapid mountain river,
The centuries cannot stop her running.
All of us are involved in this whirlwind…

ТВЕРДЯТ БЕЗ УСТАЛИ ВСЕ О ТЕБЕ, ДУША

Твердят без устали все о тебе, душа,
А где ж от глаз ты прячешься сама,
Чтоб отыскать, поди, сойдёшь с ума,
Философов всех перевороша.
Бездонно море, нет в нём берегов,
Сестра её родная – смертна плоть,
Наверное, зерна нам не смолоть,
Не отыскали ещё нужных слов…

— © Adolf P Shvedchikov, PhD

Everyone Says Tirelessly About You, The Soul

Everyone says tirelessly about you, the soul,
And where do you hide oneself from the eyes,
It is easier to become crazy than to find you,
To turn over of all philosophers.
Bottomless sea, there is no shore,
Her native sister is mortal flesh,
Perhaps we cannot grind grain,
Not yet found the right words…

— © Adolf P Shvedchikov, PhD

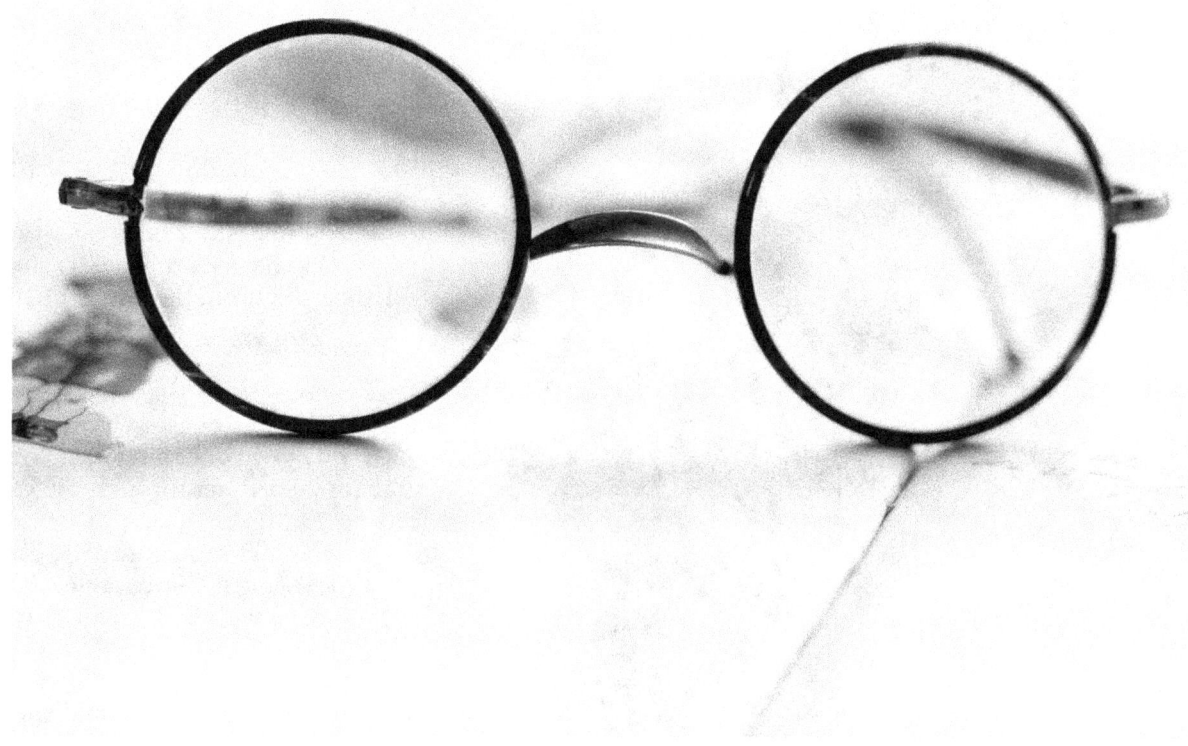

The Whispering

I must reveal the secret being address
Satan knows it's the only way to confess
Let the River Jordan rush across time
Looking for words that never rhyme
On bended knee with heart and soul in hand
Mortal calamity of evil caused by a woman

Eden was a paradise of earthly bliss
Satan knows the fairer beings weakness
John the Baptist washed away sins grime
Disciples on a mission committed the crime
A serpent smile and juicy apple in her hand
Human knowledge ushered in ticking sand

Addressing the agonies of a world gone
Secrets nested and locked are not won
The shackled imprison blood and soul
The dark woven webs a never let go
Demon shadows rain like snowflakes
Whispering wicked deeds until mind breaks

— © Gary A Drury

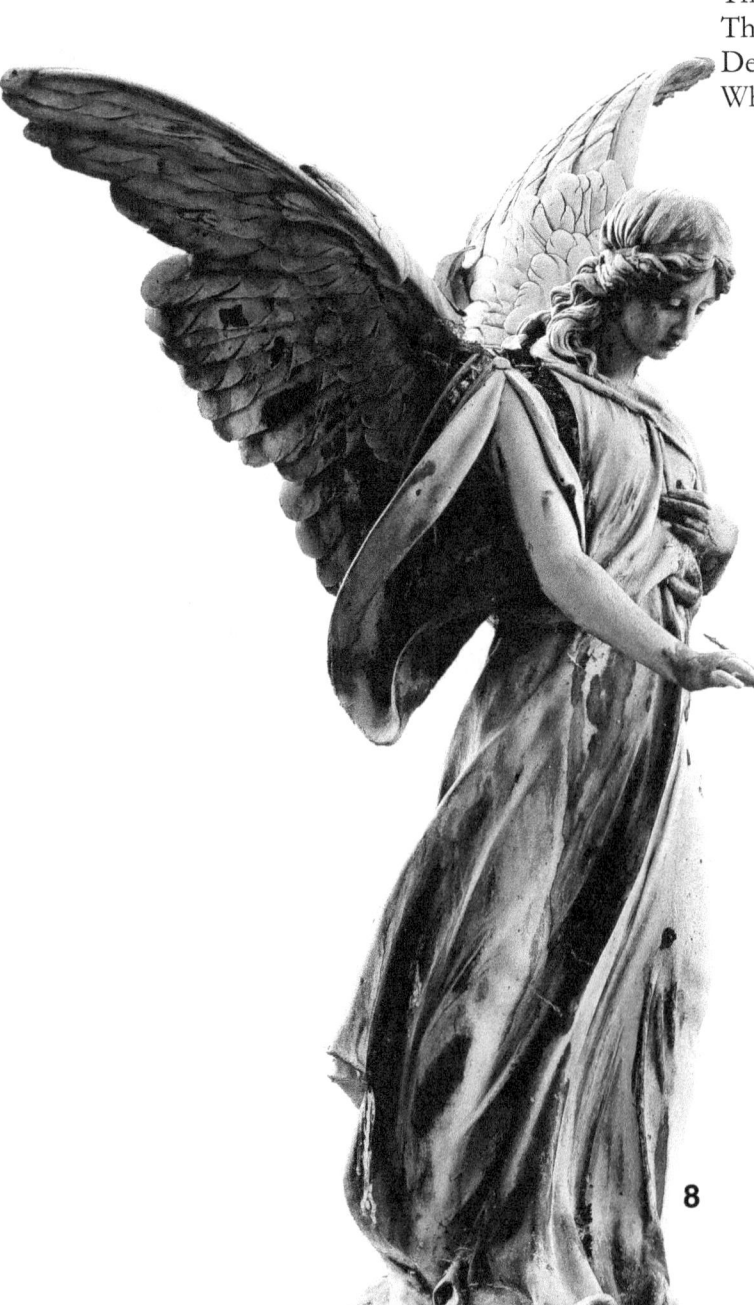

On Wings of Hope

When life has not been kind to her
as she goes through each day,
she rides upon the wings of hope
to help her on her way.

These wings of hope are always there
to chase away her fears,
by giving her a sense of peace
that's helped her through the years.

These wings are sent from God above
and give her strength each day,
to cope with life and all its trials,
by chasing blues away.

Without these wings what would she do,
to cope with pain and strife?
They give her strength to carry on
and live a peaceful life.

— © Sheila B Roark

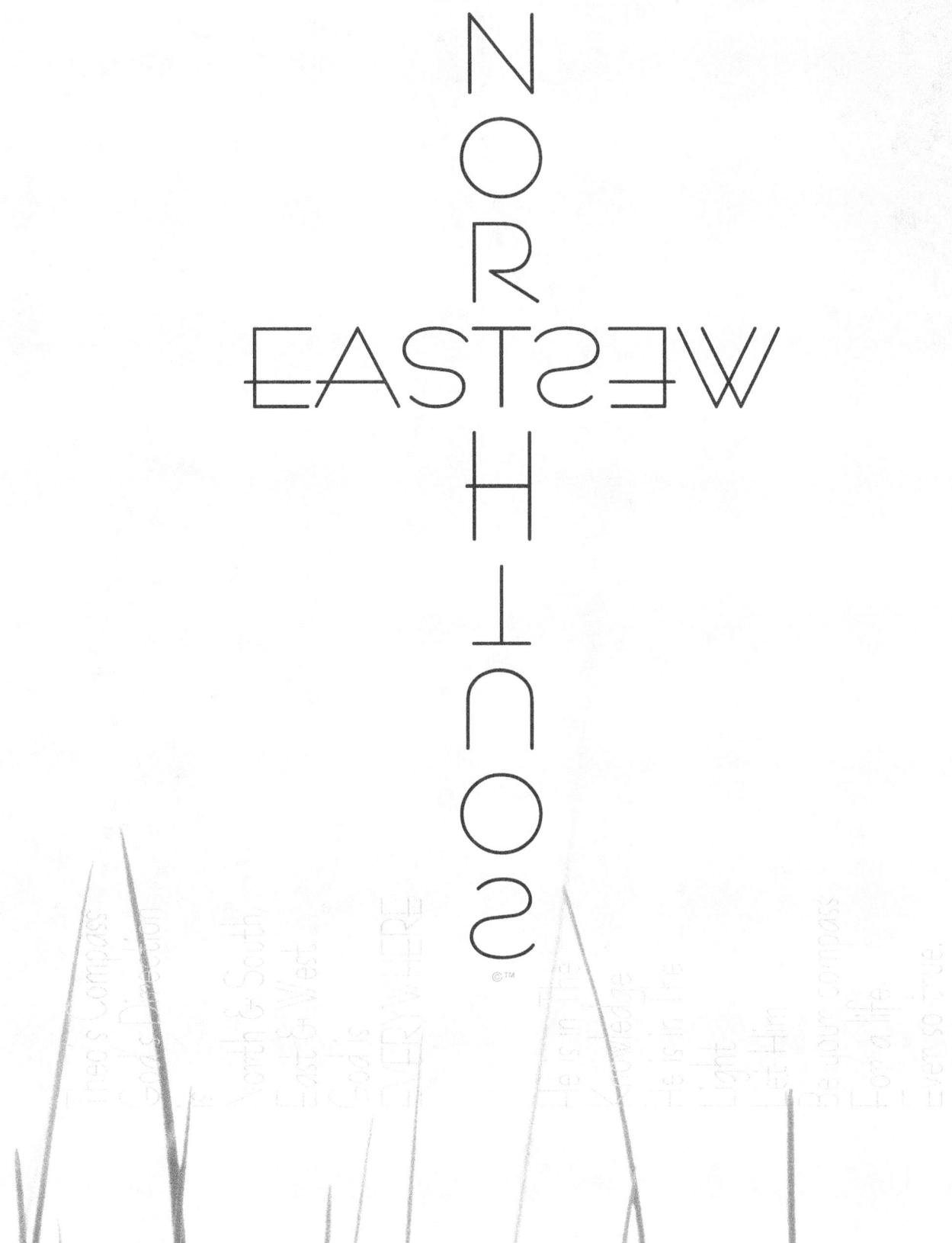

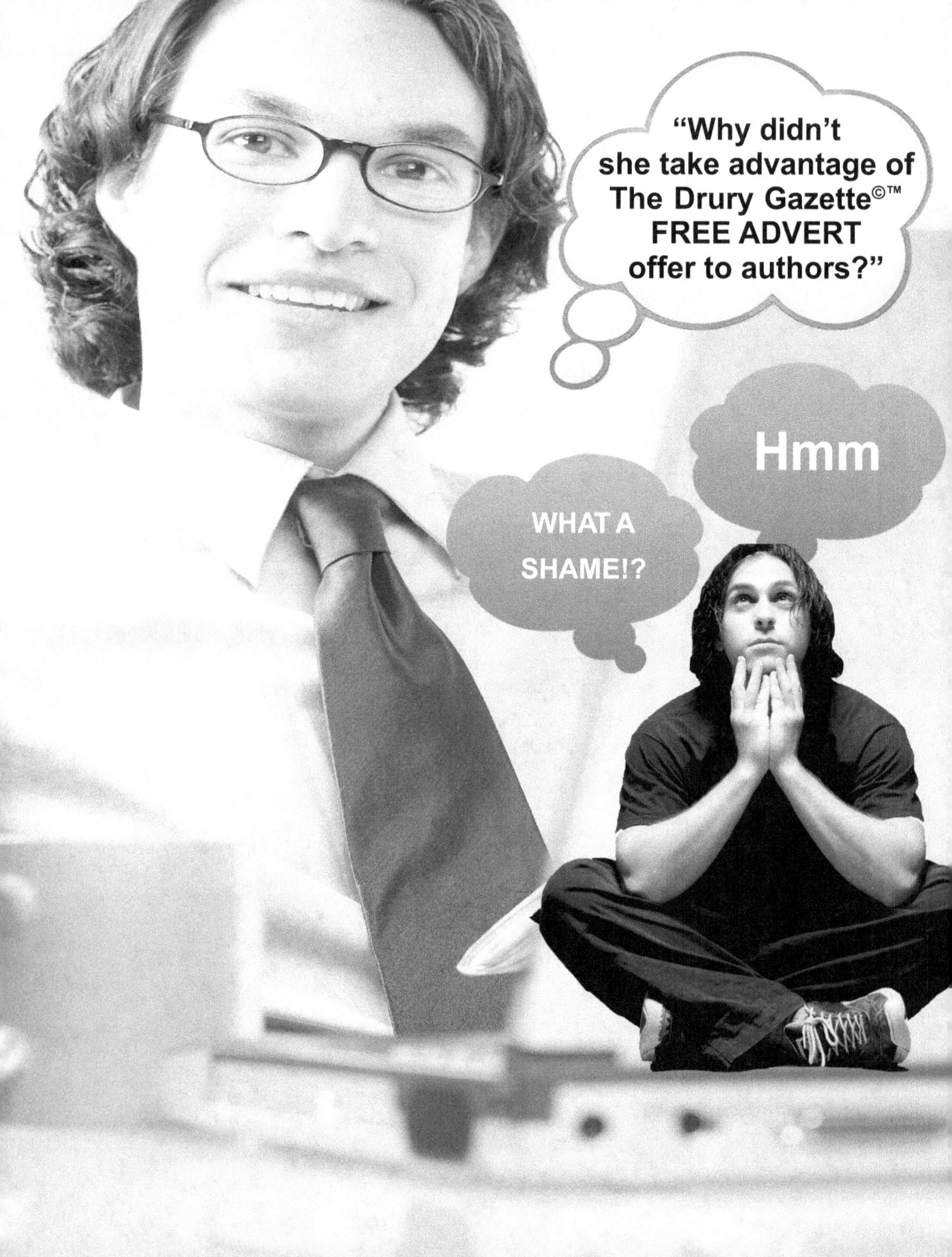

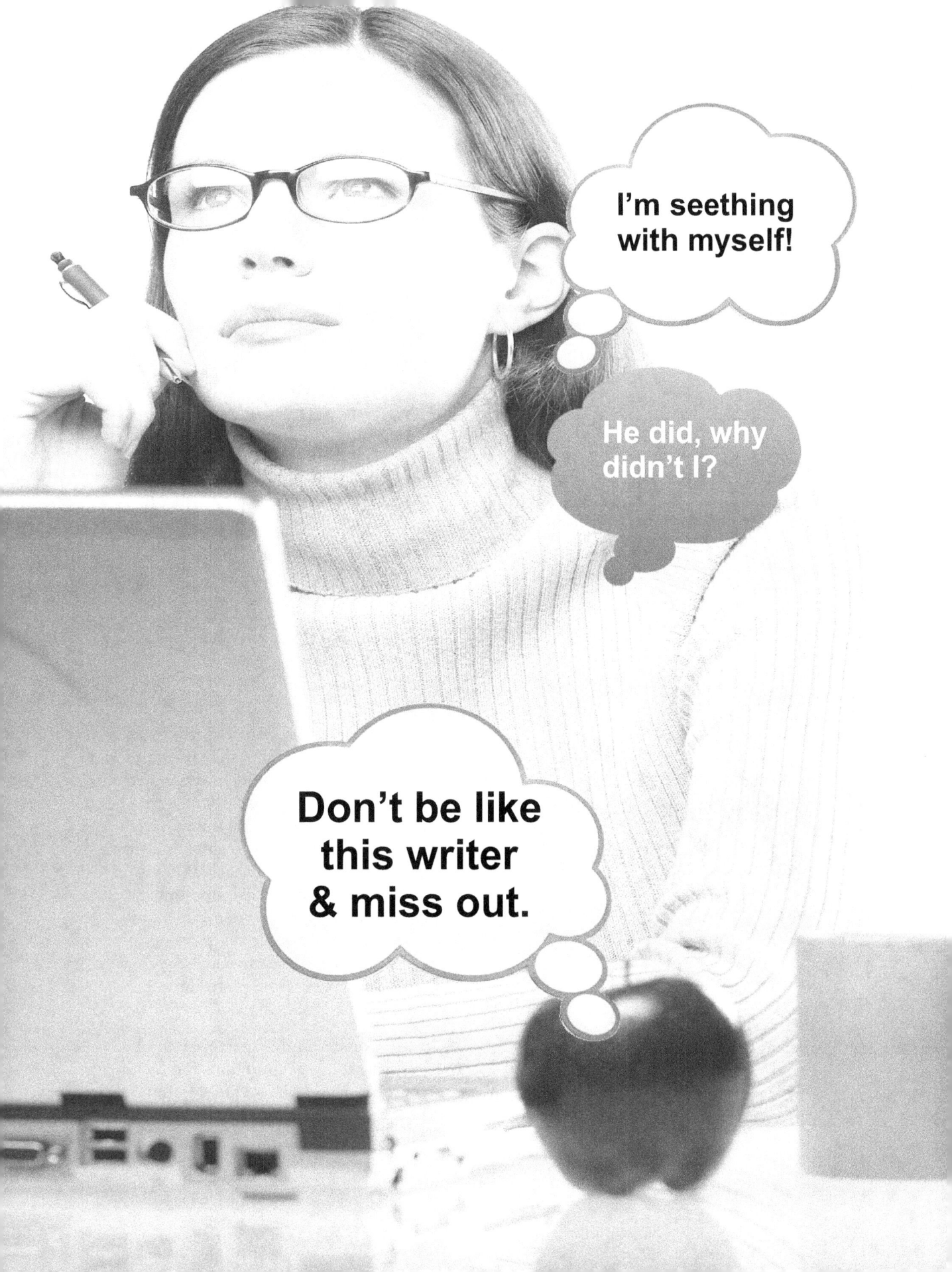

Surviving the Battles

by Dr. Gerry Drum

Multiple Sclerosis is also known as MS can go unnoticed and undiagnosed for a myriad of years. Nevertheless, the symptoms present themselves early but generally dismissed by the individual due to his or her hectic lifestyles. Multiple Sclerosis requires a medical diagnosis as it causes several different symptoms, includes vision loss, pain, fatigue, and impaired coordination. Sometimes muscle spasms, also referred to as myoclonus is a sudden jerking, quivering, or twitching of a muscle, which may last a few moments or several minutes in duration, however, it seems to go away on its own. It is not uncommon for such a sensation to reoccur randomly. The symptom severity and duration does vary from person to person. Some people can remain symptom-free most of their active lives, while others may have persistent severe chronic symptoms for life.

Consequently, a person with other existing medical conditions can be ninety-percent more likely to develop multiple sclerosis later in life. People diagnosed with epilepsy are predisposed to the increasing percentage to develop the ravages of multiple sclerosis. Although, never verbalized to me that there was a link between the two. Of course, I was primary school age and the neurologist spoke mostly to my parents. What limited time I had one on one with my doctor was merely for him to enquire a few additional questions. Later, I continued visits to the neurologist during college due to inconsistencies of university life. Still, nothing was mentioned regarding the correlation between epilepsy and multiple sclerosis.

Unbeknownst to me at the time of enduring plethora testing, blood work, computed tomography (CAT Scan), etc. I had the world-renowned neurologist specializing in epilepsy. The neurologist's words still resonate in my ears. I was defiant and refused to take the prescribed medications which didn't last long as I was the child. My medications were never accurately regulated, as I was a zombie when I'd ingest them. The medications for the type of seizures I experience didn't cease them. Once, I was an adult I quit taking any medication period. Eating God in the greens with His love, remaining as organic as humanly possible these days I manage very well.

Now, that a plethora of years has elapsed, I have taken time for some research. It is apparent that epilepsy and multiple sclerosis are linked closely together with more commonly than by mere chance. It's almost inevitable not to have one without the other. I have experienced over several years' duration blurred vision, temporary blindness, spasms and twitching in lower leg muscles. Tingling numb needle-biting in the feet and legs, which were not persistent and generally, the interval was less than five minutes. Nonetheless, those moments of moderate to severe pain have been reasonably infrequent.

Should want to know more Goggle Epilepsy and Multiple Sclerosis symptoms and you'll discover why it can take several years for a proper diagnosis to determine a course and treatment regiment to commence.

Epilepsy and Multiple Sclerosis are equally common conditions having a judicious chance of occurring in the same person. Studies have completed which conclude the two are practically inseparable. I am blessed not to endure the severity that one or both of these ailments can cause. However, I know of others that have multiple sclerosis that began slowly and accelerated quickly making his or her natural body alien to them. And the active lifestyle once sported is now a distant memory that fades away like a forgotten dream. One such individual fighting her ongoing battles with positive optimism to conquer the multiple sclerosis war with God's strength to carry her is featured in this publication.

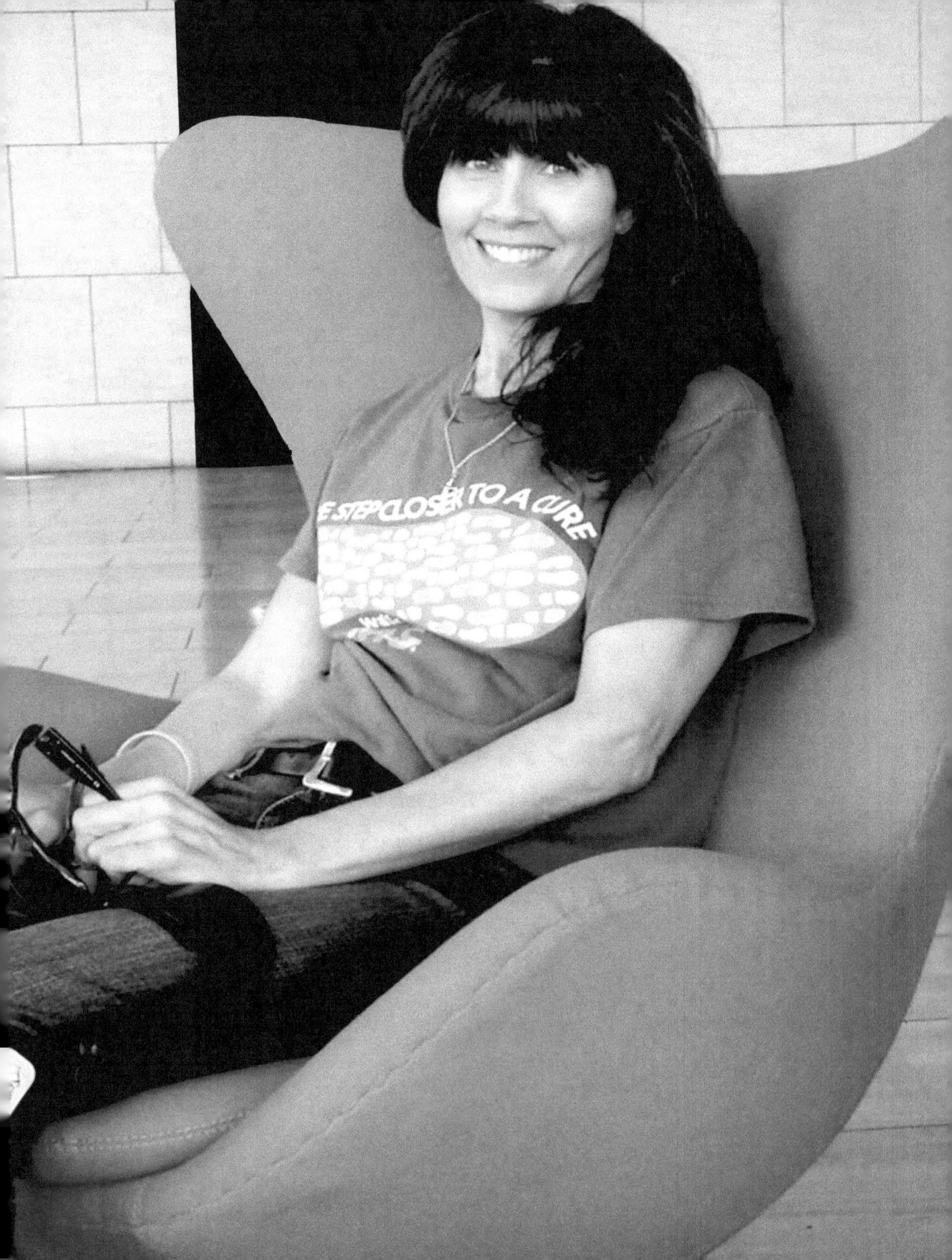

FEATURED PUBLISHED WRITER

Mary Ann Cincinnati

Dancing with Satan
TRUE STORY
by Mary Ann Cincinnati

Uncertainty is our only guarantee each day we live. We never know what life has in store for us. We can acquire an illness, be in a car accident, or hit by a truck. Now with all these shootings, it seems there's one a day.

Our minds scrabbled with a cocktail of questions. What is this world coming to? Why is this happening? Where are the preachers with how this correlates with scripture? There is so much unfocused hatred. It's miserable that we can't feel safe anywhere, not even going to the movie theater, a concert, or an errand to Walmart.

Nonetheless, I am now middle-aged, multiple sclerosis is hammering profusely that life can terminate any minute. I'm seriously concerned now, I have children. This may sound eerie, but I ponder the effect it will have on them. The effect multiple sclerosis will have on my entire family. Will I have the fortitude to fight each step of the way as the stages progress and worsen? My courage wanes the instance I contemplate the future. Actually, I definitely worry that their father may pass before I do. It would be positively devastating. He is the one, the foundation, knowing exactly what to do when it comes to our girls' needs. He is reliable, responsible and the one that provides for them. I am, unfortunately, physically unable to do what is necessary for me as a mother, a wife, and as a person. I can be there for emotional support, nevertheless, I'm a failure, I cannot be their rock physically. My mind remains strong nonetheless my body is invalid. Their father, being an orthopedic surgeon, bears a tremendous amount of stress. Consequently, he has family burdens compounded on top of that, not just our kids but other relatives, also.

I know all of this is such a concern these days due to my deteriorating health. February 17, 1996, it all began, on what should have been the happiest day of my life, our lives, when I gave birth to my first child. The presumptuous planned memories of motherhood would immediately halt. She was a high-risk pregnancy. This made her birth all the more special bring her to term. The fairy tale life I wanted to give her smothered in hugs, kisses, and love. When my daughter was six to nine months old, and we were on the floor playing, suddenly I could not move my leg. My left leg paralyzed. I called my husband promptly to please rush home, but it seemed he was ready to depart just as soon as he was present. Now that I deliberate about it in retrospect, I can't believe my spouse being in the medical field didn't consider I needed a doctor appointment for an evaluation. Of course, that's the downside of being married to someone interning to be a physician, they are certain everything is a figment in your head. Moving on . . .

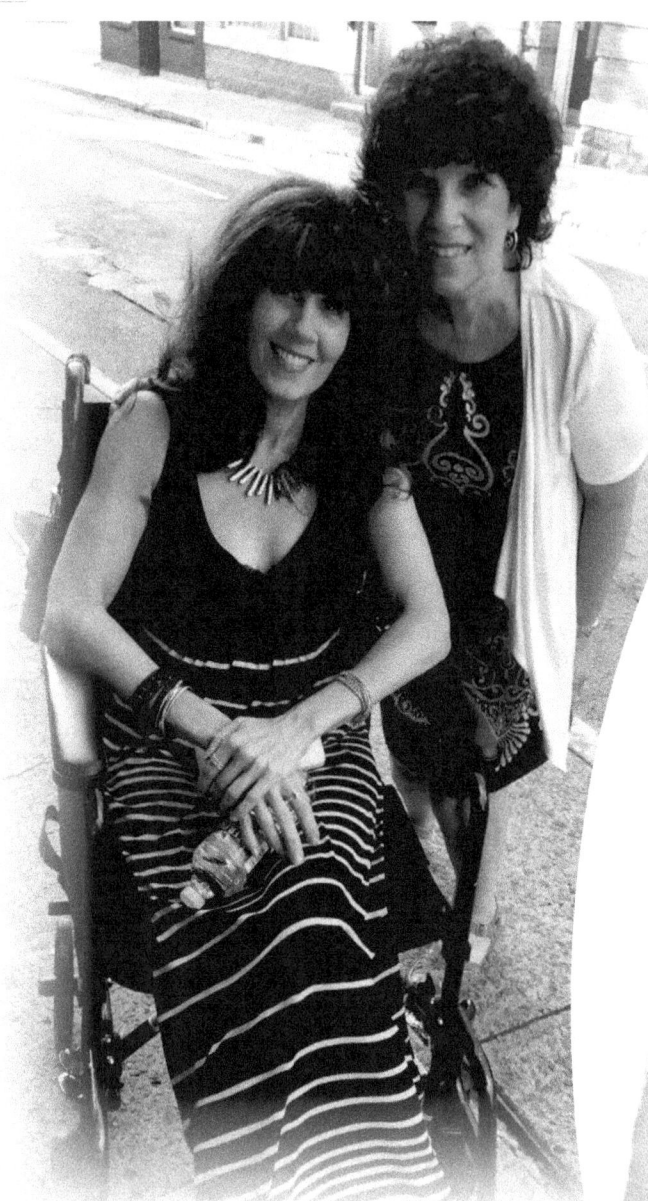

Mary Ann Cincinnati

with sister Joann

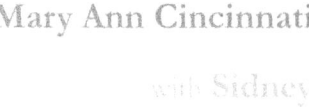

Mary Ann Cincinnati

with Sidney

Consequently, the summer of 1999. My husband and I took our firstborn daughter to Dutch Wonderland in Pennsylvania when she was a toddler. Her memories are vague today, but I recalled it like yesterday. A joyful memory that would spoil due to my questionable health. Instantly the life seemed extracted straight out of me. Enormously exhausted, I remember as if it were mere minutes ago. It was an abnormal feeling beyond any experiences before. I had told my husband, his arrogant remark was, "SUCK IT UP." He showed no sincere concern of a loving spouse, I felt tiny about an inch tall. He provided no comfort or moral support. I could never complain about anything without his reverberating remarks always something like, "You walk a day in my shoes." I'm in agonizing pain and tortured by his offhanded comment. Oh, how that would burn right through me! Clearly, he hadn't the slightest clue what war I was battling. He couldn't have cared less.

Ordinarily, I'm a very active, energetic person that would walk the dog briskly every day. Highly resilient, I'd take the blows and bounce right back to give whatever another shot. I realize now that the sensation in my left foot was merely the start of a foot drop. A small introduction to what was waiting ahead of me. Several years later when I went to the gym, after a duration of time passed and I was getting off the leg machine, my legs would become lifelessly feeble. Not tiredness from a vigorous workout weak, but entirely much different. It was so wicked that I needed the aid of someone to walk me to the car. As I hadn't the forte to leave on my own accord. Eventually going to the gym would be another activity to store away in the past.

The sunset rises every morning long before the alarm sounds to begin another trying day. The mystery remains and I still have no thoughts, suggestions or a solution to what is wrong with my body. One day while exercising at home, vision in my left eye went blurry. From a clear focus to indistinguishable images, vague merging colors. This was indeed disconcerting that I may be losing sight. "What more could possibly go wrong?" I queried in my thoughts. Lord knows I cannot voice it verbally in this house. Noticing the same fogged vision happened when I showered as well. Additional doctor visits weren't pacifying me. I need a direct, definitive answer. I knew to be careful about what I wished for. But I'm exhausted and frustrated living in this limbo of not knowing. Months later, a doctor of significance with a solemn expression painted on his face spewed the dreadful news, that I had multiple sclerosis. Multiple sclerosis, the words rang inside my ears, however, the brain couldn't absorb the information, it didn't want to. Trying hard to push those nasty words out of my head, and back into the doctor's evil mouth. Regrettably, it was far too late, the seed planted and the roots took hold. My life literally ceased as every emotion one can experience sank to the depths of hell at the pit of my stomach. I must regurgitate, but multiple sclerosis embedded in every fiber of my being had taken residence. I couldn't expel the horror. "Is my life over? My emotions were a mixed bag of anxiousness, anger, disbelief, frustrated, hatred, self-pity, and unknowing what to feel. Never will I take for granted even a day or a fraction of a second. If only this could be a horrible mistake. A nightmare from which I will wake."

After the diagnosis, however, I continued working, but my disease progressed. I attempted to carry on life as usual and enjoy my family. Faith was questionable, why would God punish me. Feeling alone, abandon and receiving no emotional support put a substantial strain on the marriage. I was angry and eventually felt hopeless. I didn't even want to live any longer, but knew, that wouldn't be justifiable

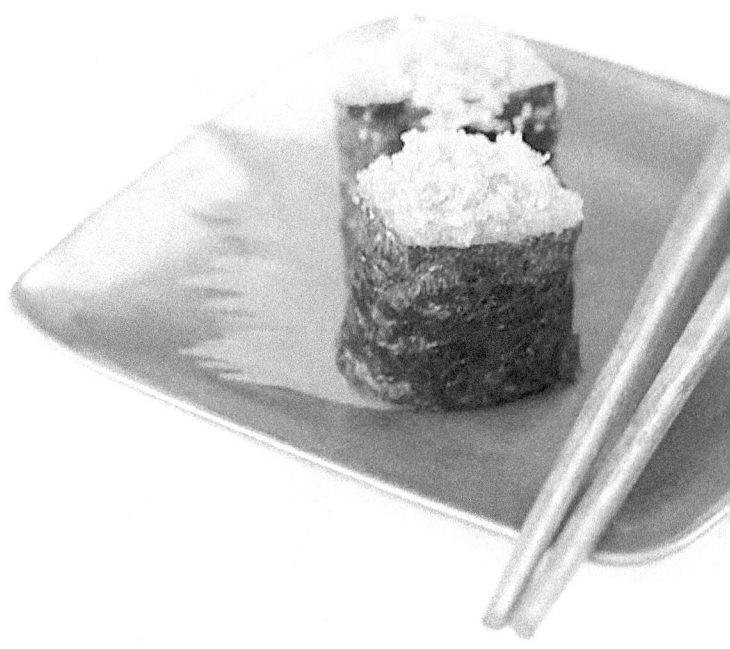

to the girls if I did something deplorable. Considering how it would have such a negative effect on them and their future. How dare I ponder depriving the girls of their mother when my mother expired when I was nineteen. My children are twenty-one and twenty-four years of age.

Currently, I'm in the process of writing a book 'Dancing with Satan' to share my personal journey, wanting it to inspire others out there struggling with this malicious debilitating disease to trust and have faith in God. To know they too can have a life after being identified with multiple sclerosis. The Lord was all I had to lean on during the trials and tribulations and I continue to do so now. Those of us with multiple sclerosis must represent our color *orange* showing integrity, strength, and endurance. We don't merely survive each day, we live! That is what the color orange represents to me and to the world. I'm showing this unforgiving multiple sclerosis whose the boss. You can also. Stand up with me and demonstrate to every disease crippling us that one person can cause change, bring progress toward a cure and eradicate it from existence as we have poliomyelitis (AKA polio), smallpox, and other plights!

I felt nothing, feeling nothing made me feel better. I lost interest in doing anything, had no motivation. I had forsaken interest in the living period. Then the girls took my thoughts and I finally started leaning on God after dealing with this debilitating disease for so long. They depended on me even if I wasn't one-hundred percent there. It was ruining my life, devastated contemplating losing this battle. If I can't win the battles I can't possibly win the war. I must muster up the courage if not for myself from this depressive state but for my family. Consequently, I wasn't giving in to multiple sclerosis. My story won't end here if I have any say in the matter by God's saving grace.

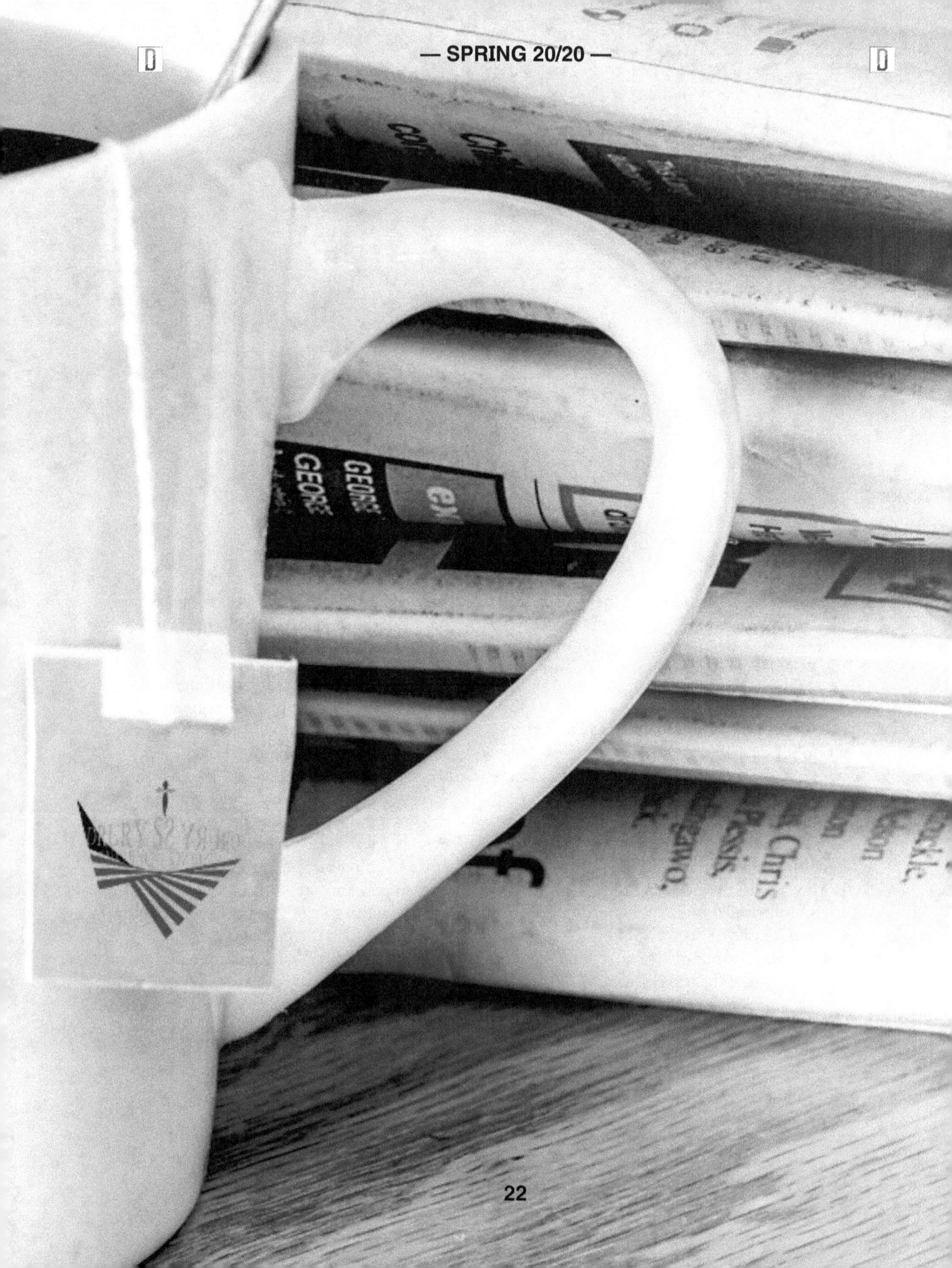

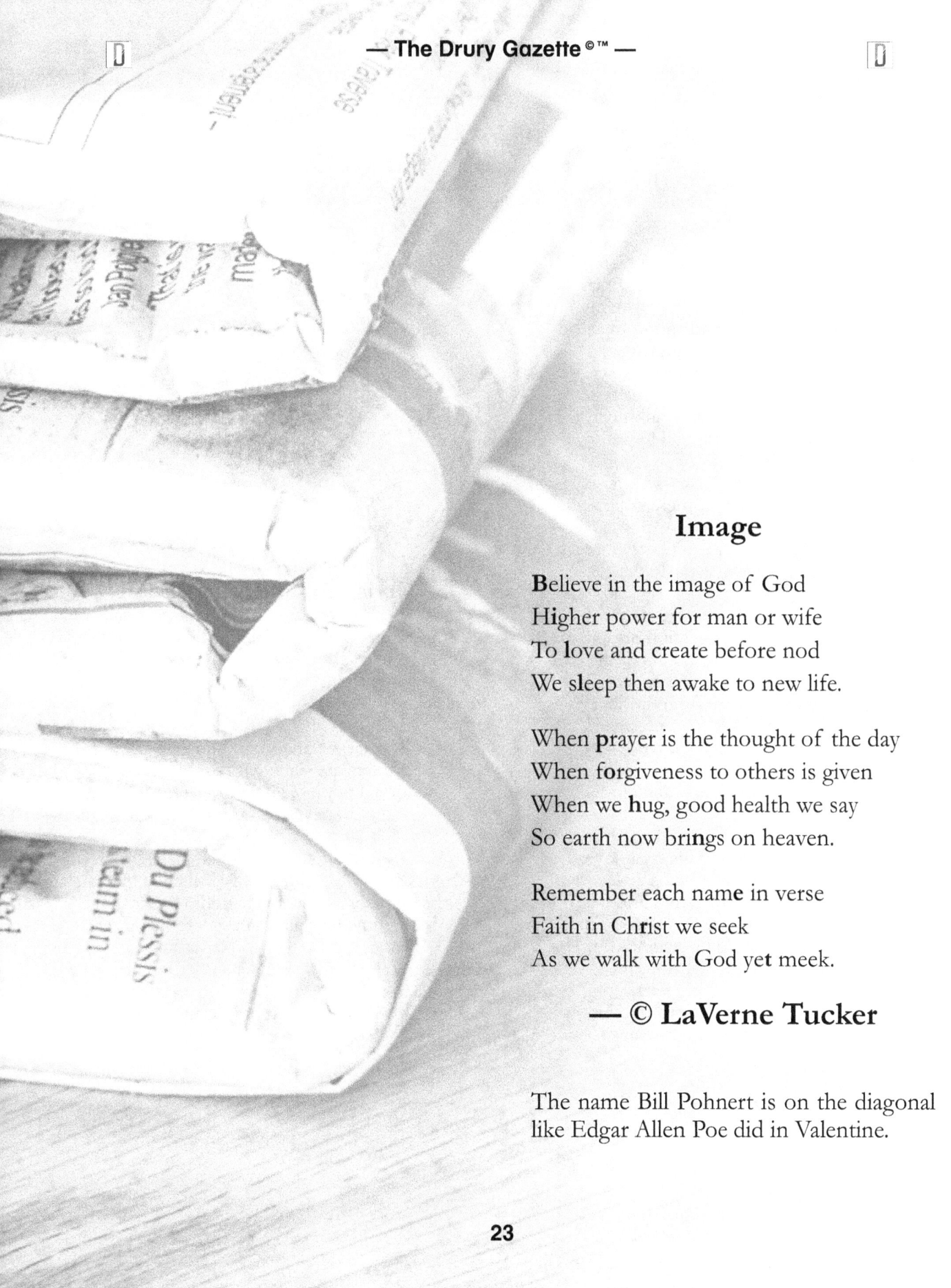

Image

Believe in the image of God
Higher power for man or wife
To **l**ove and create before nod
We s**l**eep then awake to new life.

When **p**rayer is the thought of the day
When f**o**rgiveness to others is given
When we **h**ug, good health we say
So earth now bri**n**gs on heaven.

Remember each nam**e** in verse
Faith in Ch**r**ist we seek
As we walk with God ye**t** meek.

— © LaVerne Tucker

The name Bill Pohnert is on the diagonal like Edgar Allen Poe did in Valentine.

A Place

I'm searching for a house of God
where He is welcome first
a place of total truth for which
I hunger and I thirst; where
the Spirit moves and speaks to those
whose hearts already won,
the believers' true inheritance
abundant life found in the Son.
With hearts full of thanksgiving
eager to worship and to praise
in the freedom of the Spirit
voices singing, arms we'll raise.
Please tell me that there is a place
a house of God, of prayer
of power, of joy on every face
and know that I'll be there.

I'll hear the awesome sermons
of his word with passion preached
in the power of the Spirit the
hardest of hearts will be reached
Where the fire is on the altar
and his holy presence fell
his Spirit moves the music
the sanctuary then to swell,
with all the praise and glory
he is so worthy of
as his people rise to thank him
for his grace and his great love,
for you know of such a place
his house that you could lead me to
I remember there was once a time
when I would be leading you,
my heart is oh, so heavy
I've been searching for so long
for that holy place to worship
and sing my great Redeemer's song.

— © Janet Goven

Christmastime Compassion

Atmosphere swelling rendering all to compelling
to keep in their hearts everywhere they did go,
the love in receiving, the joy in believing
the message of peace so the whole world would know.

Cookies are baking, decorations remaking
carolers are singing on every street,
popcorn is popping, neighbors are stopping
to share and declare kindness, and mercy shall meet.

White snow is falling while families recalling
the gifts and the memories of Christmases passed,
time not forsaking, stitched into the making
of a lifetime to quilt, each square being cast.

with the goodness they find when the families unwind
have hearts that respond to hearts needing to sing,
give them the gift of yourself, not what's found on a shelf
the blessings that Christmastime compassion will bring.

— © Janet Goven

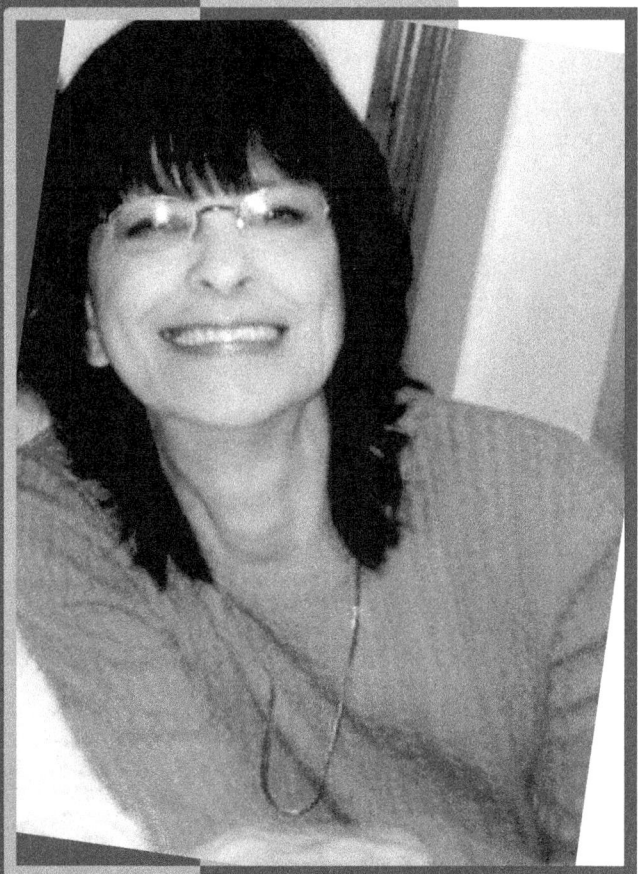

My Broken Heart Still Sings

The ground beneath my feet
begins to crumble
the rope, so strong, worn down
to a few strings
my reality was shattered
in a heartbeat
but let me tell you why
my broken heart still sings.

He has a name that is
above all others
He's Lord of lords and coming
King of kings
the only Son begotten
of the Father
Jesus, the reason why
my broken heart still sings.

Set my feet on solid rock
now I am standing
the rope replaced with His
everlasting arm
my reality now has a purpose for
His kingdom
He keeps me safe from Satan's
wiles and intended harm.

Jesus is the reason why
my broken heart still sings
I feel his presence always
in the blessings that he brings.

— © Janet Goven

The Weather Is Changing

I feel the changes coming
for spring is on its way
with flowers dressed in brilliant hues
that brighten up our day.

The air is now much warmer
surrounding blooming trees
inviting all the flying birds
to enjoy the passing breeze.

Springtime is a busy time
when baby birds are born
and little squirrels play games of
tag from early in the morn.

Yes, I can feel the changes
of springtime on its way
when all of nature comes alive
to brighten up our day.

— © Sheila B. Roark

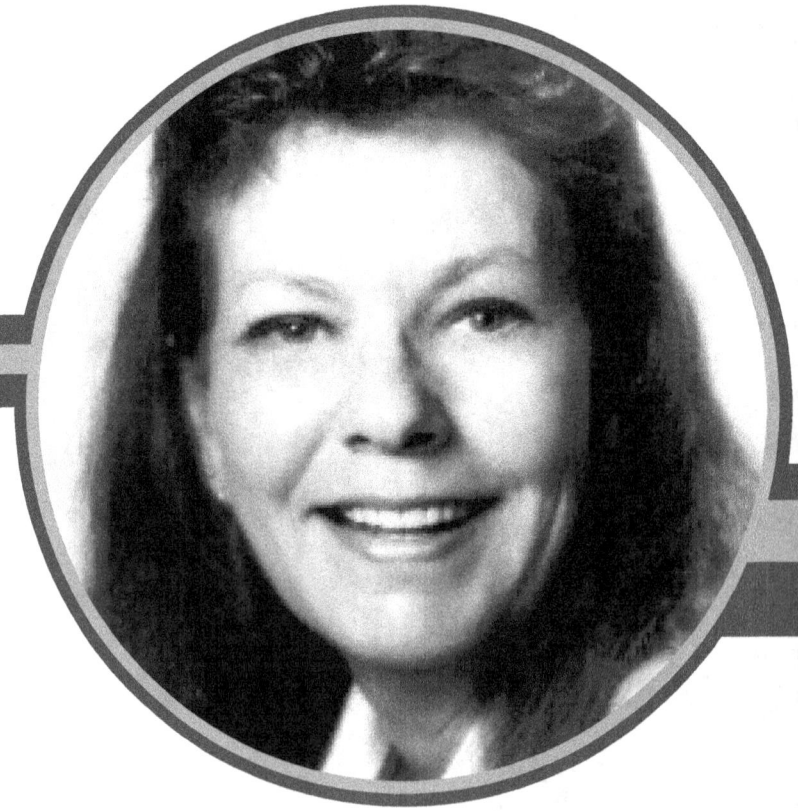

Colors of the Seasons

January is the start of the year
colored white from the snow,
and glimmering with large icicles
as winter breezes blow.

Spring has many colors
from pastels to dark green
provided by all nature
in this season so serene.

Then the summer comes again
lit by the golden sun
shining brightly with its rays
that glow till the day is done.

And finally, it's autumn's turn
to share its rustic hues
and paint the world so brightly
as we enjoy the views.

Each season has its color
from rustic red to white
so we can all enjoy this gift
so filled with spiritual light.

— © Sheila B. Roark

Where Were You?

For years we were such close friends
sharing good and bad,
but now I feel so all alone
along with lost and sad.

Where were you when my husband died
on that awful night?
Leaving me to cry alone
through the blackness of the night?

You tell me I'm dramatic
and I'm too much for you
so you can't be there at this time
to help me battle through.

So now I cry big salty tears
and feel as cold as stone
because my friend has gone away
as I sit all alone.

— © Sheila B. Roark

CASINO

by Diana Kwiatkowski Rubin

The Atlantic City casinos were hot and smoky, with many hopeful gamblers at the Roulette and Black Jack tables, still, others playing slot machines. The sounds of clicking and clacking coins resonated throughout the atmosphere. It was crowded along the corridors. Too many people bustling along, seeking food and drink, excitedly talking while scheming their next moves.

A small, frail blonde sat at the penny machines, trying her luck, pressing the various line buttons and frowning, without having much success. Pushing through the crowds, a heavy man with a deeply tanned and lined face, rolled alongside her in his wheelchair.

"You're not doing it right, here, let me show you," he said, "You have to play thirty lines at once. It greatly increases the odds."

The woman was taken aghast, somewhat unnerved by the portly stranger.

She meekly replied, "I guess I don't know what I'm doing."

"Naw," said the loud man, "you just need some guidance. Here, I'll show you.

My name is Joe, by the way."

"Matilda pleased to meet you," she replied.

"So Matilda, have you been in Atlantic City long?"

The woman bashfully answered him. "No, it's my first time. I am here on a bus trip from my church."

"Oh, well, it's your lucky day. I am a regular here. I own one of the local restaurants. The best way to win is to keep trying and never give up."

"My funds are somewhat limited. But I am trying to play the penny slots."

Joe laughed and said, "I think you need to try a better machine. Follow me, I will show you one of my personal favorites."

At first, Matilda was taken aback, but then she thought about it. Her luck wasn't very good, but maybe if she could actually win some extra money, her lot in life could improve.

Joe ushered Matilda throughout the crowded casino floor to a more remote, private room behind the game tables. The place was almost deserted, except for two other lone souls who quietly sat before large slot machines with flashy lights and designs. They robotically fed their dollars into these machines, and the machines would ring and buzz, with carnival type of music notes as they won the cash.

Matilda was amazed.

Joe told her, she too, could now try to win some major cash.

"Just pick a machine," he coaxed her. Matilda opened her battered purse, and she took out several rumpled bills. She inserted them into the machine.

"More.... more! That's not enough! The more you bet, the bigger the winnings!" he urged.

Matilda bit her lip, embarrassed, and pulled out several other rumpled bills.

"Now you're really gambling," Joe shouted.

"Place your bet, take a deep breath and believe that everything is about to change for you," Joe encouraged her.

Matilda squeezed her eyes shut and dreamed that everything would be different . . . yes . . . this time her life would really change.

She pressed down hard on the button, her head swimming, and her heart racing.

Suddenly, there was a deep, deafening sound and all the lights started flashing, music blaring and chimes ringing. She felt true fear, an excited but nervous thump in her chest. Then everything went dark.

No one saw Matilda ever again, though Joe was frequently a visitor, rolling along in a wheelchair, talking to total strangers after introducing himself and asking them to join him in his private gambling room. No one knew why these people never surfaced. Perhaps they won big? No one knows but Joe himself, and maybe Matilda, but they are not about to tell what luck, both good or bad, brought their way.

Perfidia

Oh, how fickle, faithless,
Disloyal, and yes even
Treacherous we members
Of the human race can
Be, and sad to say all
Too often are, yes we're
Coffin bound wound up
In our web, we weave
To deceive with an eye
To receive betterment in
This world of unsettlement.
Desire fires our hearts,
souls and minds
To travel a path of
Blind falsehoods that
deceive us into believing
The end justifies the means
For our greed and lust
To make us bust
The trust that breaks
The heats of others.
Oh how ruthless we are
To the toothless who
Cannot bite back.
The lightning and thunder
Of Perfidia will never
Bring back the
Garden of Eden again!

— © **Gerald Heyder**

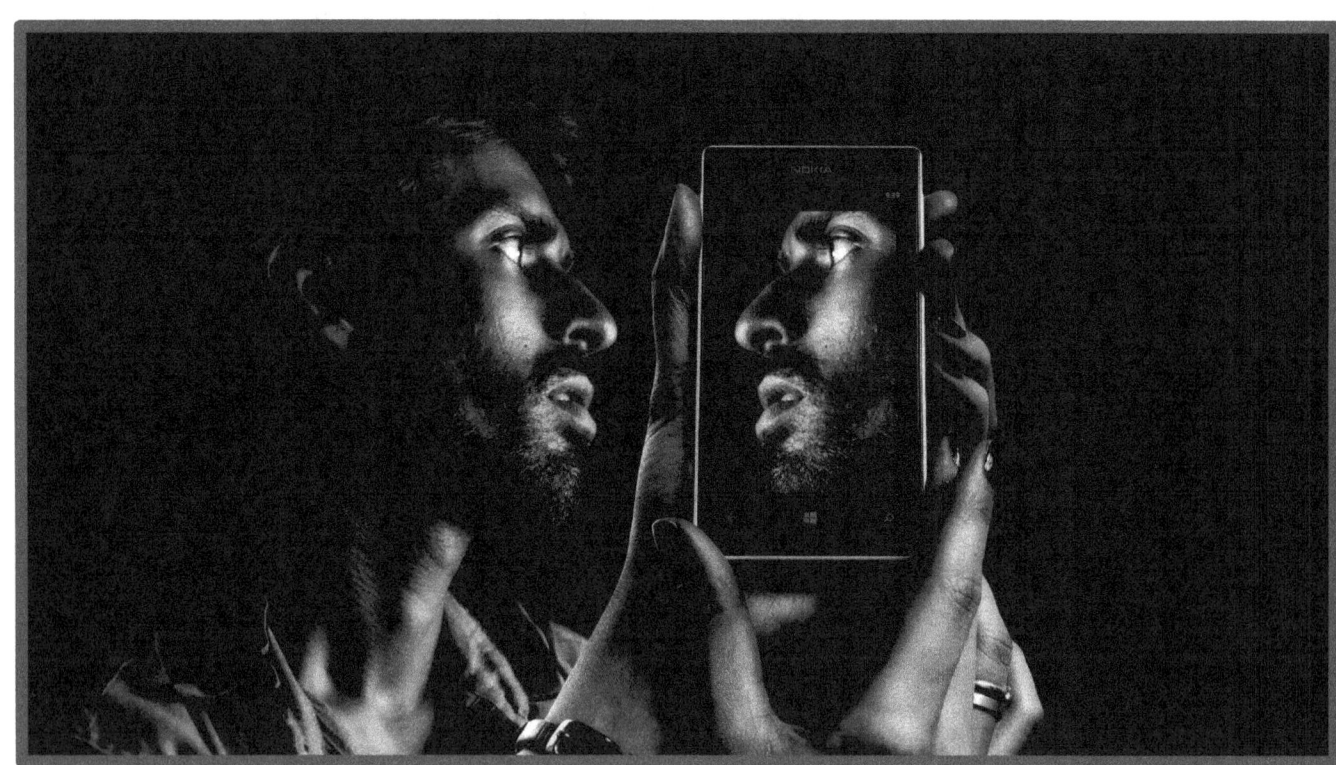

Photo by Gerd Altmann, provided by PixBay.com

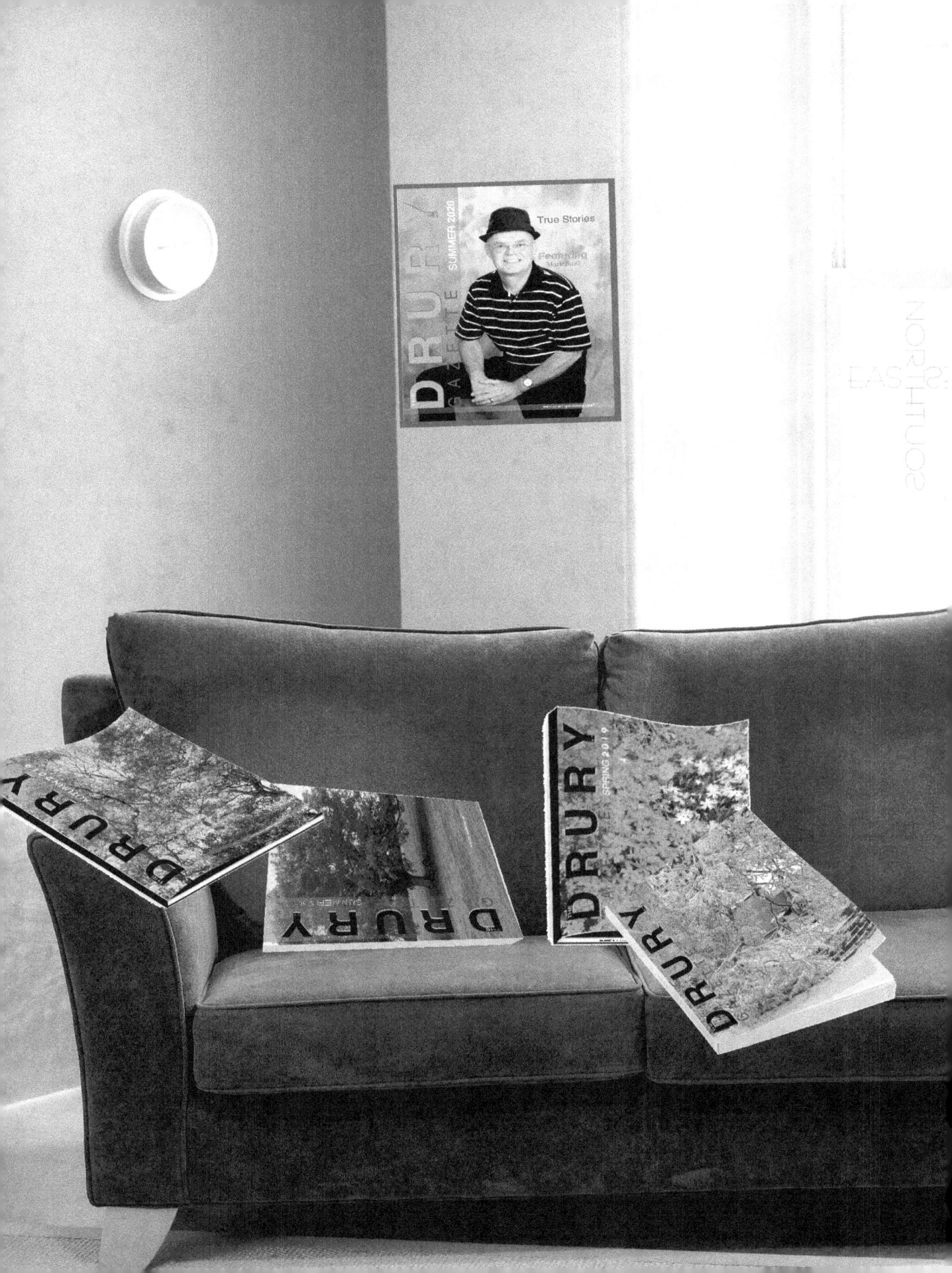

The Market SQUARE

Click the authors' photo will take you to author website or author page. Clicking on book covers usher you to trusted vendors. QR Codes available, scan with Android or iPhone to be directed to websites for additional information or purchase the author's book.

Click ↑, Get $10 Off
When placing your first order or use
CODE: GDRURY31E0

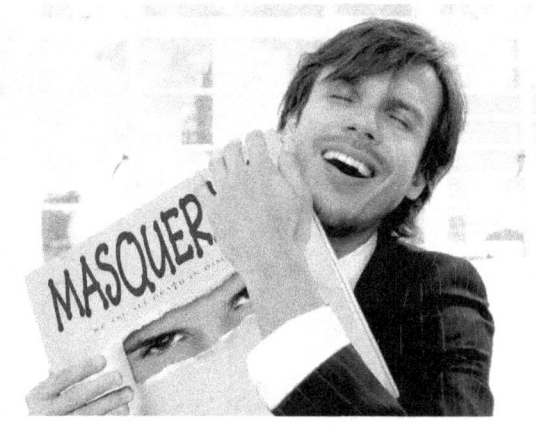

Wandering Boots
Appalachian Trail Adventure Tour
407-234-1209
info@wanderingbootsadventuretour.com

The Authors Lounge

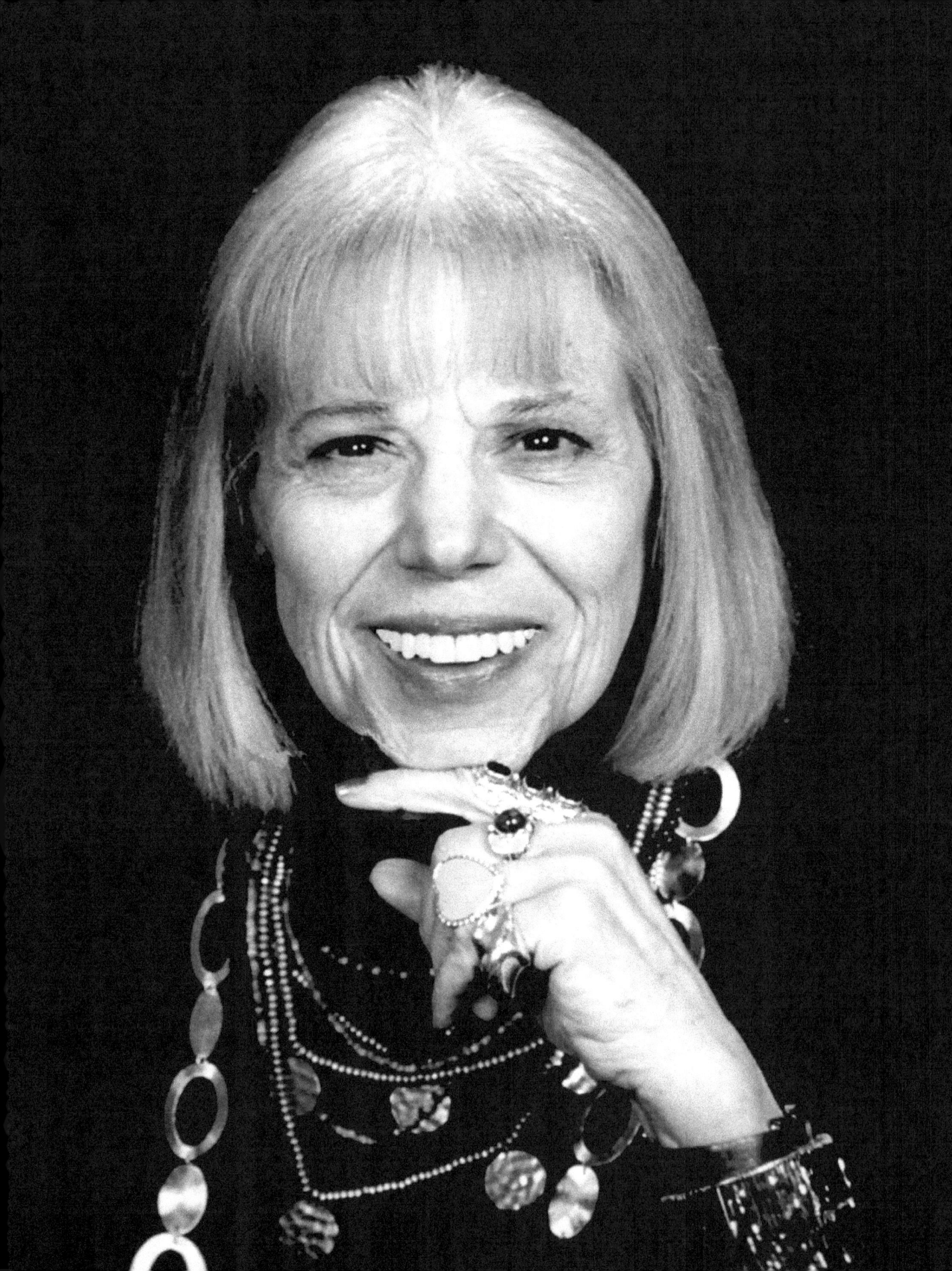

Susan C. Barto

was born on June 21st, 1941 to enthusiastic parents Eda and William Forcellon. She later married Harry W. Barto with whom Barto had a son William M. Barto. Barto received her educated at Katherine Gibbs School, Union College, New Jersey, Seton Hall, New Jersey. She has enjoyed extensive travel to Egypt, France, Italy, and England. Barto has worked as Legal Secretary, Legislative Aide, and Writer for the last 20 years. Her memberships include Past President Friends of the Hunterdon Museum of Art, Director of Volunteers at the Hunterdon Museum of Art, New Providence Library Board, New Providence, New Jersey, Raritan Valley College Book Group. Susan C. Barto's personal accomplishes are being married for 41 years to a loving husband, Harry, who died in 2001. Her only child, William, who died in 2000. Barto says *"I love to write. Writing defines who I am."* Barto's exhausting list of publishing credits briefly mentioned here is Drury Publishing©™ Anthologies and The Drury Gazette©™, Creative with Words, Writer's Guidelines and News, and Yesterday's Magazette.

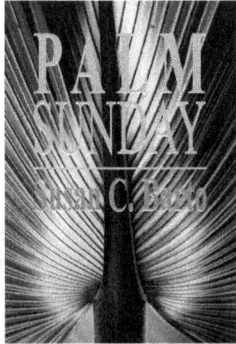

Palm Sunday

A saga about an Italian American family growing up in Brooklyn. The story follows the adventures of this large warm family as they move from Brooklyn to New Jersey and some as far as Florida. However, no matter how far the family is flung from each other they gather each Palm Sunday and Christmas to celebrate the holiday and more importantly the family. The story centers on five female cousins and how they grow and prosper-their loves, joys, and sorrows. The story moves between the present time and the past telling of their parents and grandparents and how the family came to this country. The story concerns the grandparents and parents and their lives and fortunes and the children who in turn grow to have children and even grandchildren of their own. Each Palm Sunday and Christmas the family members reconnect and join together sharing their lives. ISBN-13: 978-0-9770533-9-1 Pages: 64 Type: US Trade Paper Trim Size: 9" x 6" Language: English

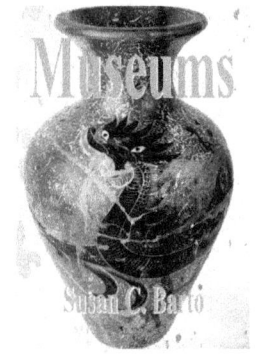

Museums

Museums are beautiful peaceful housings for history in all eras. Places to enjoy where we have been, where we are, and where we may be in the future. Museums spark our imaginations and creativity because of its wealth of mystery we are eager to explore. Why not visit and experience the museums of an author's mind as well. Open your thoughts up to another perspective. ISBN-13: 978-0971251625 Pages: 64 Type: US Trade Paper Trim Size: 9" x 6" Language: English

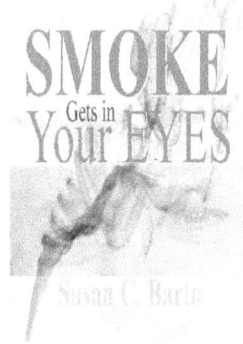

Smoke Gets in Their Eyes

The new conglomeration of short stories by Susan is outstanding. Rush and get your softbound copy today before it's too late. Smoke Gets In Your Eyes by Susan C. Barto is a group of short stories about life, love, marriage, and family. The author delves into a myriad of aspects of love and relationships between spouses, children, and lovers. Some of the stories seem to reflect the pain and its subsequent growth as the protagonist comes out on the other side. One story tells about Emily Dickinson as the author imagines her and what her life and emotions may have been like. Other stories are more prosaic describing the love between husband and wife as they interact with each other and their offspring. ISBN-13: 978-1438245508 Pages: 68 Type: US Trade Paper Trim Size: 9" x 6" Language: English

Excerpt from Palm Sunday

Harry was the only prize Susan ever won. Their meeting started as a fluke when Susan's best friend, Maryann, called just twenty-four hours before New Year's Eve to see whether or not Susan wanted to go on a blind date for the big evening. Maryann knew that Susan had fought with her boyfriend the night before, and therefore, remained dateless.

"He won't like you as he's studious and serious, and you're a flake."

"Maryann, you know what you can do with your blind date," Susan rejoined. At this juncture Maryann's steady, Pete, interrupted with "Of course he'll like you—a sexy terrific girl like you."

Since Pete's blarney never failed to crack Susan up, she relented with a laugh. "Okay, I'll go, but I'd rather stay in my room re-reading GONE WITH THE WIND and listening to Frank Sinatra's "In the Wee Small Hours of the Morning" while the strains of the party my folks are hosting drift up to my room."

Susan's reluctance to go to the party—

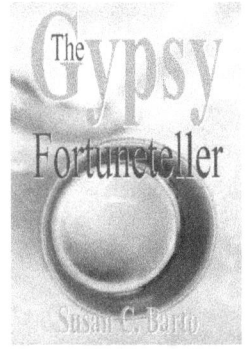 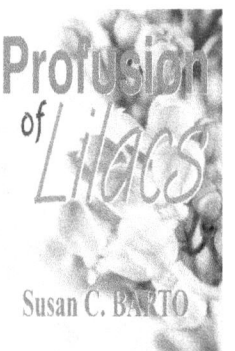 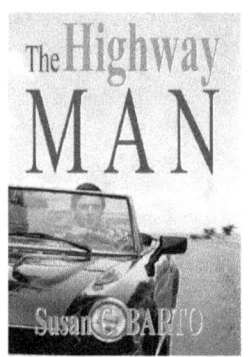

The Gypsy Fortuneteller

What the future holds only the Gypsy Fortuneteller can convey to you. Hmm In this riveting collection of short stories. ISBN-13: 978-0971251687 Pages: 108 Type: US Trade Paper Trim Size: 9" x 6" Language: English

Profusion of Lilacs

A Profusion of Lilacs leaves an invigorating scent in your mind. Via tales of fiction casually intertwined with real life. ISBN-13: 978-1494218683 Pages: 186 Type: US Trade Paper Trim Size: 9" x 6" Language: English

The Highway Man

The Highway Man is a riveting collection of short stories. ISBN-13: 978-0971251694 Pages: 104 Type: US Trade Paper Trim Size: 9" x 6" Language: English

Note: After the loss of her husband and son Susan C. Barto Drowned in loneliness and despair which contributed to her Losing 175 lbs. Harry and Bill were her entire world and they Loved her equally so. Writing was her refuge, her therapy, her Salvation.

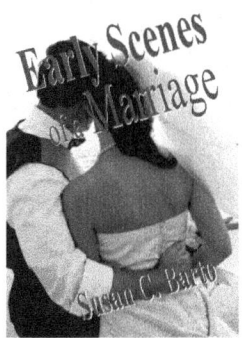
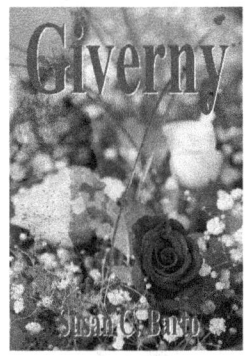
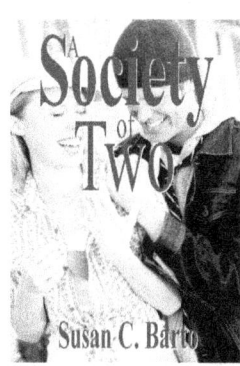

Early Scenes of a Marriage

Giverny

A Society of Two

The early years are the best, that only gets better as time moves on. Highs and lows are a normal course of life or is it? ISBN-13: 978-1493774081 Pages: 28 Type: US Trade Paper Trim Size: 9" x 6" Language: English

Beauty and Mystery are in the eye of the beholder. What wonderful worlds await in the shadows. ISBN-13: 978-0971251649 Pages: 74 Type: US Trade Paper Trim Size: 9" x 6" Language: English

When two people are one, one world, they are the society. ISBN-13: 978-0971251656 Pages: 64 Type: US Trade Paper Trim Size: 9" x 6" Language: English

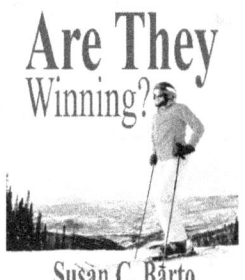

Are They Winning?

Chances are they might be winning depending on your definition of winning. Then again, we may never know. ISBN-13: 978-0971251632 Pages: 56 Type: US Trade Paper Trim Size: 9" x 6" Language: English

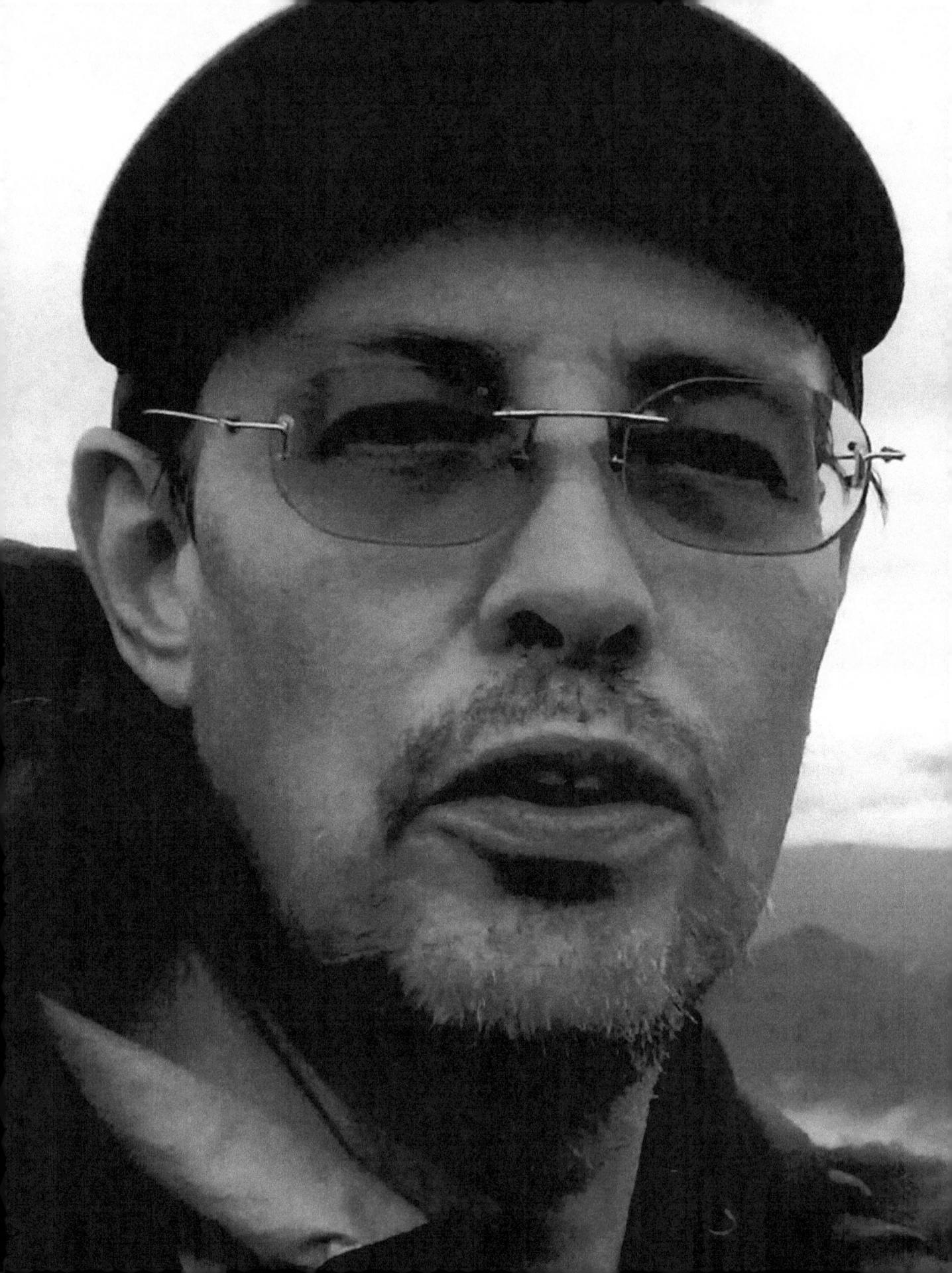

Gary A. Drury©™

writes books, considering where you're reading this, makes obvious sense. He's best known for writing poetry and non-fiction. He publishes a free quarterly gazette promoting writers. He's an avid supporter of free speech, traditional & independent-publishing. . . . Drury subscribes to the philosophy that everyone has the inalienable right to bear arms. So, grab pen and paper and start writing it's our most powerful weapon.

Kentucky Clay

A plethora of azure sky and cotton clouds
Drift freely across mountainous mounds
Striking vivid imaginations ravenously ablaze
Floating aimlessly in a causal dream like daze

We are two sail boats adrift aimlessly
Sailing toward the other on a vast sea
Our lighthouse beacons us to golden shore
On our journey kismet bounds us forevermore

My love is just like Kentucky clay
Once it sets and stains it does not wash away
That is the way I felt when you came
Everything I ever wanted was in your name

I found my home in good ole Kentucky clay
My heart palpitates hard like Kentucky clay
I found my love in red soil Kentucky clay
I'm made of that ole fashion Kentucky clay

— © **Gary Drury**

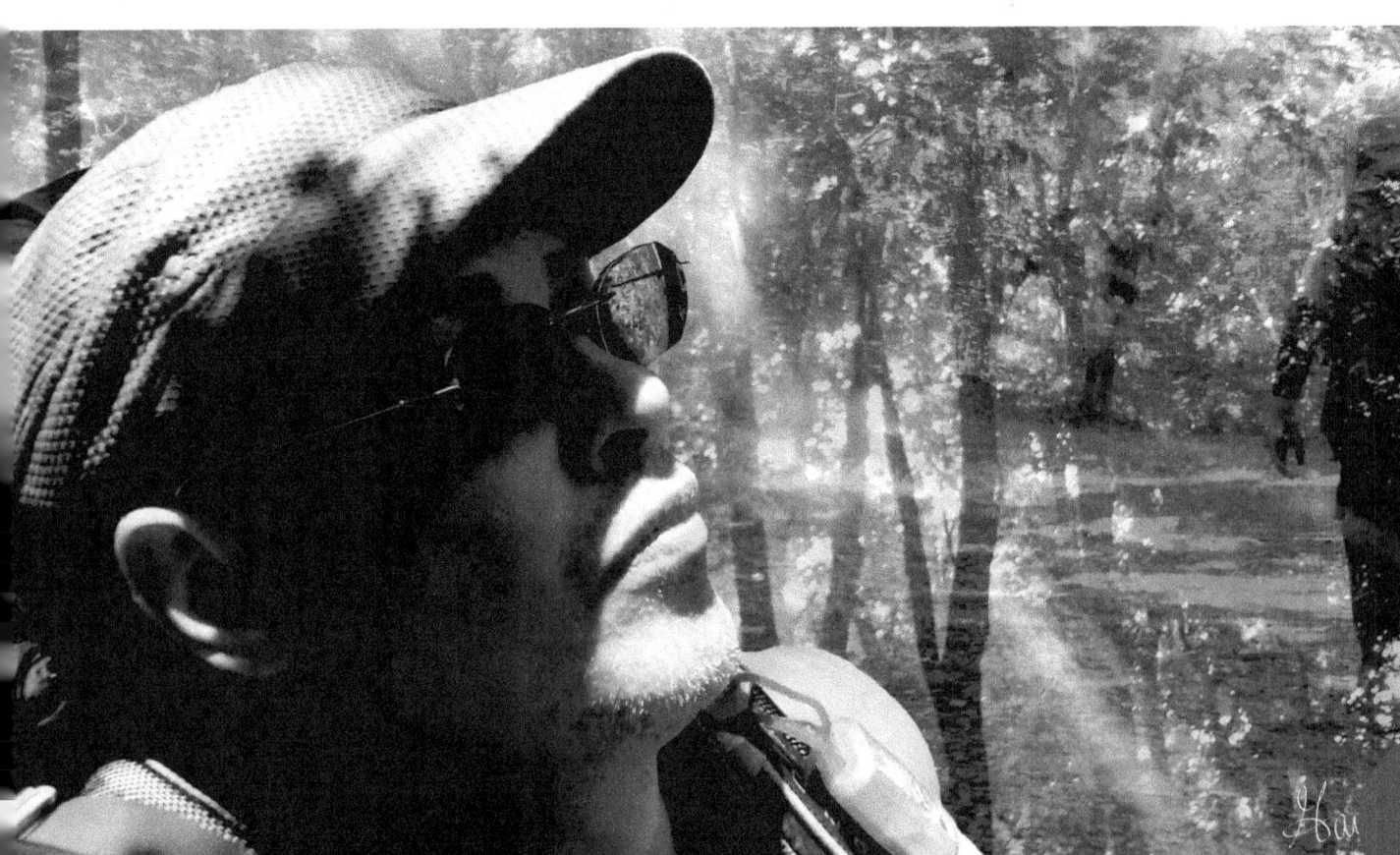

Light

Born unto hands of fate
Whether soon or late
Each man must perish
Greet his grim reaper
Implore favorable destination
A noble honorable just soul
Holds kiting glory
A nefarious rogue harden soul
Warriors for peace eternally
Righteousness harbors
Neutral ground
Leveling consequences
Equally and justifiably
Where faith resides
Lovingly in engrossing heart
Each man must harness
Strength despite tribulations,
Overcome inconceivable odds
Light shall pierce darkness
Blazing path to true freedom
Whether soon or late
Each man must perish
Discovering his darkness,
Discovering his Light.

— © **Gary Drury**

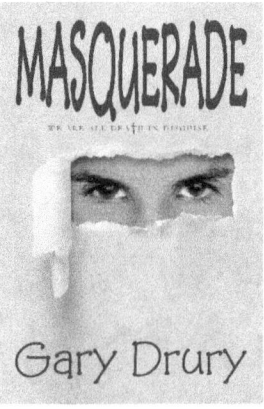

MASQUERADE is a tantalizing collection of poems reflecting on daily experiences, circumstances and mere creativity. A compilation of work spanning several years, it is a poetic excursion expressing a conglomeration of the author's thoughts, which convey a simplistic sense of honesty. The dark, vivid imagery of an observant soul has molded these poems. The poems featured here are in tune with the writings of Edgar Allen Poe, by whom the author has long been inspired. The author endeavors to inspire the reader in ways he or she may never have contemplated. ISBN-13: Trim Size: 9" x 6" Language: English

CANDLE IN THE WIND is a poetry collection about God and love. The poems celebrate the Lord's goodness and show how he guides our lives. The poems show hope and faith that abound with the belief in our Lord. Some poems tell about our angels, our Guardian angels and all Heaven's angels who come to us with help and point the way to enrich our lives. The poems glorify God and give us the hope of the Resurrection and the Second Coming. The poems talk about how the love of the Lord can color and enrich our lives. Like a Candle in the Wind. the light of our Lord can show us the path to take. One poem is in praise of the beautiful four seasons of the year that color our world. One poem describes a garden and others speak of hope even in the face of the death and mourning of our departed loved ones. He sports ten authored books, Candle in The Wind translated into Russian and now available on Amazon.com. This collection of Gary Drury's newest poems should not be missed. It will enrich your library of poetry. ISBN-13: 978-1440475207 Trim Size: 9" x 6" Language: English

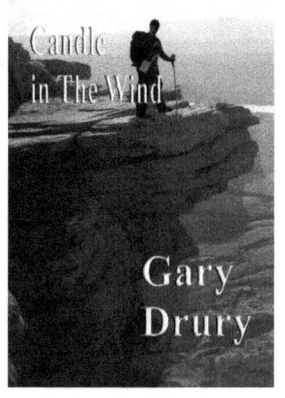

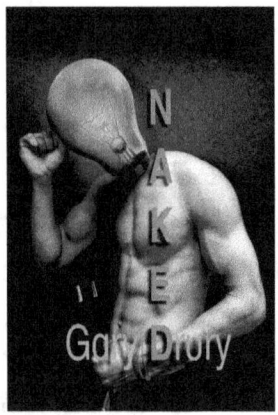

The message in NAKED is an unspoken promise life will improve, things will change, with a positive outlook, faith in your soul and love in your heart – tomorrow is a better day. Regardless of how gravely a poem may come across at first reading, the thoughts embodied the message are positive. God is answering, not with a whimper or with a roar, but silent and tame. Naked touches on sensitive subjects in today's society, such as rape, child abuse, suicide, modern relationships, and depression. More traditional poems and prose of faith, God, angels and prayer grace these pages as well. The work strives for the wellness of mind and spirit as tolerance of diversity is devotedly encouraged. ISBN-13: 978-0615949932 Trim Size: 9" x 6" Language: English

Abstract Poetry

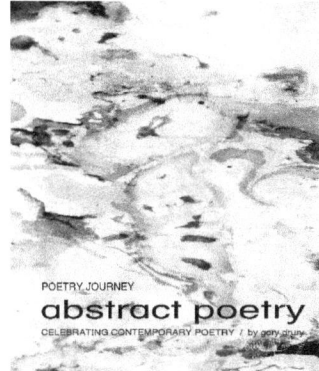

My POETRY is the absolute evolution of self-therapy cleansing mind and spirit, freeing the artist from a plethora of woes. The expressive abstract poetry blessing these pages were created using a very simple yet complicated technique I devised. Free your mind, open your eyes, permit your imagination to wonder and absorb the creativity embodied here. Poetic Beauty is truly in the mind's eye of the beholder. Enjoy! ISBN-13: 978-1985281028 Pages: 40 Type: US Trade Paper Trim Size: 8" x 10" Language: English

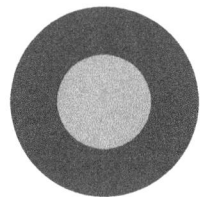 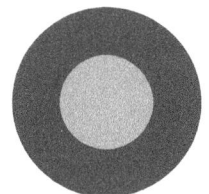 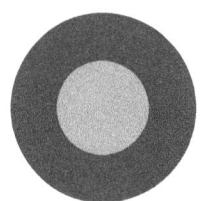

Abstract Art

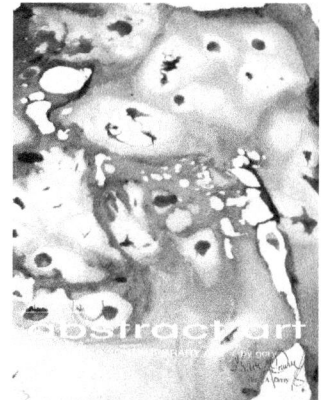

My ART is the absolute evolution of self-therapy cleansing mind and spirit, freeing the artist from a plethora of woes. The expressive abstract artwork blessing these pages were created using a very simple yet complicated technique I devised. Free your mind, open your eyes, permit your imagination to wonder and absorb the creativity embodied here. Beauty is truly in the eyes of the beholder. Enjoy! "For me generating abstract art is the liberation of my thoughts and immortal soul. A feast for my ravenous eyes to indulge and be satiated, to quench my ravaging thirst for dynamic tactile beauty. My compositions are created through spiritual thoughts of inspiration and natural phenomenon. Utilizing the simplest of tools and non-pedestrian color palettes. Rogue to the frivolous and mundane each work is incredibly expressive with explosive action and movement. Celebrating the conception of our universe, the natural surrounds, and its exotic creatures. Abstract art frees us all from the complexities of this contemporary world and permits our minds to roam unrestricted." ISBN-13: 978-1546775980 Pages: 64 Type: US Trade Paper Trim Size: 8" x 10" Language: English

Appalachian Trail Thru-Hike
Poems, Last Quotes, Photos

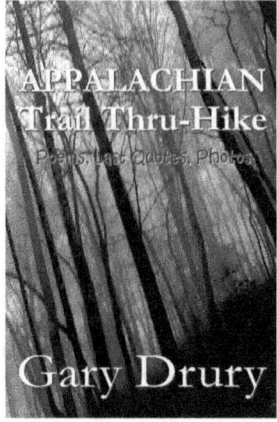

Poetry is the gateway to new found freedoms and self-discovery. It programs your mind to contemplate things a touch differently than you may have before. Much like walking in another man's shoes for a day. Books are not merely for education and entertainment. They are an opening into the author's mind and soul. Weaving into their stories real-life experiences, beliefs, political views and other philosophies. When you discover an author, poet or novelist you truly enjoy. It's because the reader relates to that writer. Poetry is a micro-story conveying its message in the simplest of form. Sometimes poems rhyme sometimes not, prose and 575 haiku's often don't. Myriad people claim to loathe poetry. However, poetry is very important in their life. Every song you listen to is a poem that has been placed to music. I'm not trying to push books that are the seller's job. But, the only way to know for sure what you like and don't like is to give writers a try. You may just discover much more in common with them. Next time you read a poem try putting some music to it and see how it reads. Not everyone is going to hike the Appalachian Trail. Not everyone wants to, not everyone is able to. But for those who would like to experience the journey vicariously, walking the Trail in Drury's footsteps as they read his words, the book will be a travel guide. Drury's book FINDING NORTH can take you to the Trail, where you'll share the struggles and the triumphs of seven months that Drury, battered in body and exultant in spirit, will always remember. ISBN-13: 978-1721670628 Pages: 48 Type: US Trade Paper Trim Size: 9" x 6" Language: English

Gary Drury shares his poetic writings with bright intensity while casually hinting admiration, inspiration, and influences of Edgar Allen Poe. This gifted author has passionately demonstrated his talent in the literary world via his originality of ideas, concepts, style, and genuine narrative technique, etc. are positively breathtaking, refreshing, nonetheless and understatement of Drury's true genius and meticulous craftsmanship with words forming his unique voice. He offers a wealth of stimulating thought-provoking ideas and delivers his message with imaginative intensity. Drury is an established author and poet.

Excerpt from Candle in The Wind

WINGS

Oh, to go where angels fly,
Where life is sweet and never dies.
Where youthful waters ebb and flow,
A place reserved for welcomed souls.
I'd spread my wings and follow the tide,
My guardian angel a be my guide.
Trials and Tribulations my worldly woes,
As my life casually unfolds.

Oh, to go where angels reside,
Where wings are never bound, or tied.
Where gentle rains fall soft and slow,
Temperatures constant and never cold.
I'd spread my wings and follow the tide,
My guardian angel a be my guide.
The sands are dripping out my soul,
Now I must leave, my story's told.

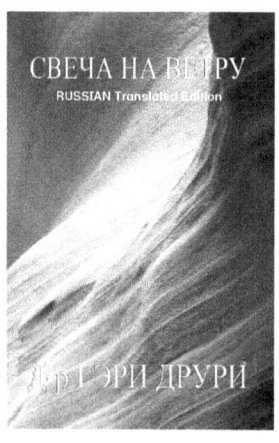

Candle in The Wind

Translated into Russian.
ISBN-13: 978-1541216693
Pages: 134
Type: US Trade Paper
Trim Size: 9" x 6"
Language: Russian

КРЫЛЬЯ

О, вознестись туда, где летают ангелы. Где вечная сладкая жизнь, Где приливают и текут свежие воды. Где всегда рады принять души. Я расправил свои крылья, следуя за приливом. Ангел указывает мне верный путь. Слежу за мировыми страданиями. По мере того как развёртывается моя жизнь.

О, направиться туда, где обитают ангелы. Где крылья не связаны и никогда не устают. Где медленно и мягко выпадают лёгкие дожди. Где держится ровная температура без холодов. Я расправил крылья и следую за приливом. Мой ангел указывает мне верный путь. Я освобождаю свою душу от песка И теперь могу покинуть вас, рассказав свою историю.

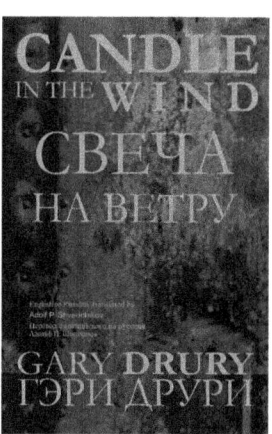

Candle in The Wind

Bilingual English and Russian. ISBN-13: 978-1987765854 Pages: 246 Type: US Trade Paper Trim Size: 9" x 6" Language: English & Russian

Color My Soul

Color My Soul is a collection of poems written over a number of years, reflecting on life experiences, circumstances and mere creativity. The poems featured in this manuscript are slightly darker, trekking the venues of love, romance, and family. The poem "My Amusement" is a lengthy piece written about a narcoleptic Edgar Allen Poe whose deepest fear was entombment while he was still alive. Edgar Allen Poe has long been a favorite and an inspiration to the author. Color My Soul is a poetic adventure expressing the author's diverse thoughts, which convey a simplistic sense of honesty. It is a compilation of work spanning several years. The author endeavors to uplift and inspire the reader in ways he or she may never contemplate to tread. ISBN-13: Trim Size: 9" x 6" Language: English

Bloodletting the Demons

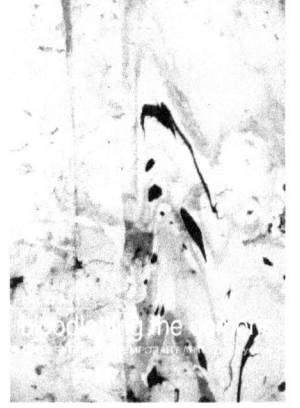

Abstract art is an explosive visual language -- chaos of hue, a thought-provoking burst of texture and form, a silent accidental arrangement. Dramatic works of art showcasing unrestrained oil paintings, construction off mental sketches. Abstract artists are unencumbered from the world around them and limited merely by their own genuine imagination. Through unadulterated instinct, composition and a tapestry of inspired color, they translate unbinding emotions of thoughts, ideas, philosophies, and personal experiences into immersive images you want to repeatedly explore time and time again. ISBN-13: 978-1456522247 Pages: 60 Type: US Trade Paper Trim Size: 8" x 10" Language: English

Releasing The Soul

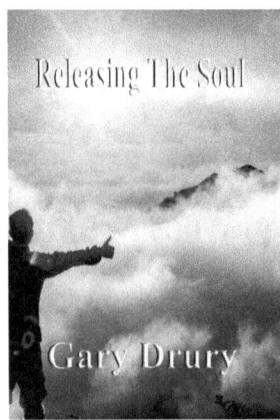

RELEASING THE SOUL is a poetry collection about God and love. The poems celebrate the Lord's goodness and show how he guides our lives. The poems show hope and faith that abound with the belief in our Lord. The poems talk about how the love of the Lord can color and enrich our lives. Like a Candle in the Wind, the light of our Lord can show us the path to take. One poem is in praise of the beautiful four seasons of the year that color our world. One poem describes a garden and others speak of hope even in the face of the death and mourning of our departed loved ones. ISBN-13: 978-1493706174 Pages: 162 Type: US Trade Paper Trim Size: 9" x 6" Language: English

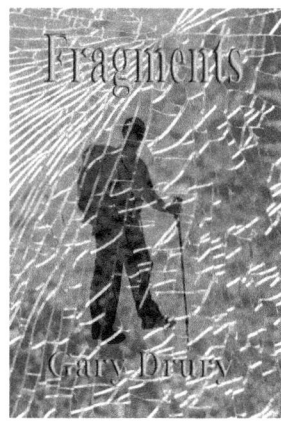

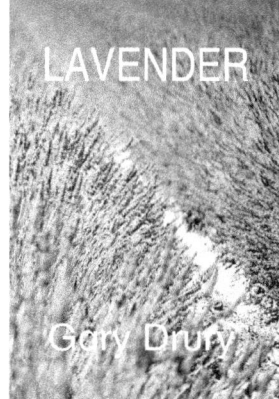

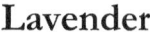

Fragments

A plethora of thoughts, subjects, and topics focusing on the strategy of faith, love, holidays, current events, etc... Perceptions of any given moment preserved on each lily white page. ISBN-13: 978-1493707782 Pages: 130 Type: US Trade Paper Trim Size: 9" x 6" Language: English

Lavender

Lavender is an uncomplicated collection of poetry of an ungeneralized nature regarding the musical connection between two kismet spirits imprisoned by moments that constitute a plethora of memories and losses leaving no regrets. Compunction resides in the ailing hearts withering from dramas storms without closure-not in the lavender. Recognition is given to the ruins of abandon fragments. ISBN-13: 978-1438242255 Pages: 74 Type: US Trade Paper Trim Size: 9" x 6" Language: English

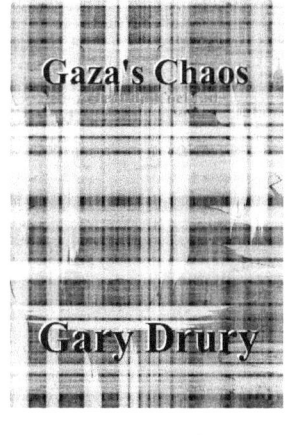

Gaza's Chaos

Gaza's Chaos (A Tequila Cocktail) represents a work touching on sensitive subjects in today's society, such as rape, child abuse, suicide, modern relationships, and depression. More traditional poems and prose of faith, God, angels and prayer grace these pages as well. The work strives for the wellness of mind and spirit as tolerance of diversity is devotedly encouraged. Cowboys Are Rugged Men inclusion herein is appropriate due to the diversity of this poetic collection and current news events. The underlining message in Gaza's Chaos is that there's an unspoken promise life will improve, things will change, and with a positive outlook, faith in your soul and love in your heart – tomorrow will be a better day. Regardless of how gravely a poem may come across at first reading the thoughts embodied in the message are positive. God is answering, not with a whimper or with a roar, but silent and tame. ISBN-13: 978-1461014829 Pages: 366 Type: US Trade Paper Trim Size: 9" x 6" Language: English

My Bad

My Bad is a compilation of poems over a period of decades gathered in this conglomeration of poetic mischief. It includes creative derivatives of angels, the hereafter, and God. A wealth of the poems deals with coming to terms with oneself and maturing into the ability to see beyond Black and White thoughts permitting the various shades an colors to shine through. It also touches upon grieving and knowing when it's time to let go before the darkness consumes, others are just a jolly mix of jest. Hopefully, the reader will discover some enlightenment and a new perspective after trekking the mental grounds of another person shoes. ISBN-13: 978-1438243030 Pages: 78 Type: US Trade Paper Trim Size: 9" x 6" Language: English

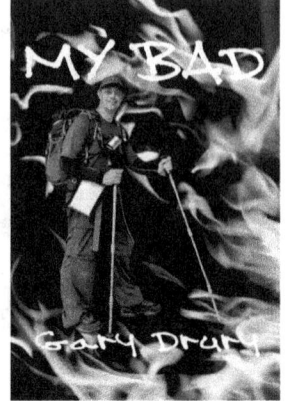

"My primary education was in parochial school where I still burden the guilt today. Not surprisingly my writings clearly convey those inner demons. Regardless of age one never escapes childhood experiences and memories. They merely shelved away to gather cobwebs and dust. Probably the reason why Edgar Allen Poe is my kindred spirit.

One year, I set out to thru-hike the Appalachian Trail stretching 2200 miles across fourteen states and seven months to complete, it's an epic journey like no other.

Here is a tidbit I'll share that isn't mentioned anywhere else as I recall. My poetry books aren't simply workings of literary art. They were designed to help me remember the plethora of passwords that continue to accumulate. My books are riddled with 'KEYS' that some may perceive as 'Typos', 'Incorrect word usage' or a name."

God, Family, and friends are a priority in his life. Then Drury's greatest joy sharing his earnest passion 'Poetry' and 'Life Experiences' with others.

Gary Drury is an award-winning writer whose publications included Candle in the Wind (translated into Russian) and Naked (his soul completely exposed). Drury's most recent books are Color My Soul and Masquerade. Most of his writings touch on sensitive subjects today. If you dare dive into his imaginative intensity.

THE APPALACHIAN TRAIL TELLS A TALE

The Appalachian Trail is more than geography that extends through 14 states and 2200 miles of challenging terrain. For poet Gary Drury, his nonfiction account of his rendezvous with Mother Nature, or, as he describes her, a "cruel, relentless mistress," the Appalachian Trail represented an epic journey. Drury is not a camper. Not a hiker. Not a backpacker, boulder scrambler, athlete, or rock climber. In order to embark on the journey that he undertook in 2014, he says, "I elected to step 180 degrees outside my comfort zone." He began the journey as a novice. By the end, he realized that he had undergone a life-changing event.

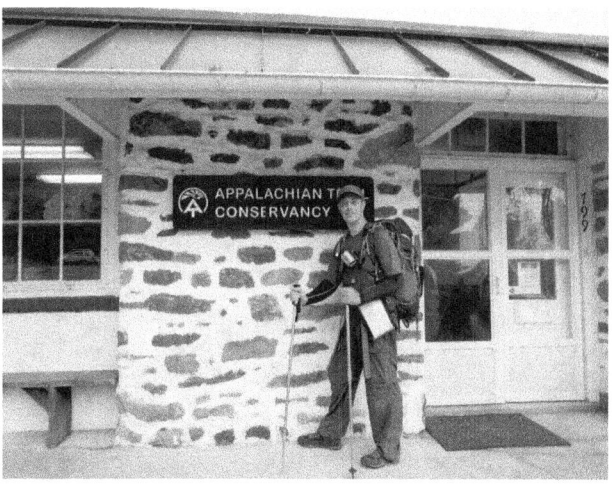

But he's a poet. So it was perhaps inevitable that he would turn the images into words when the journey ended. He's writing about his experiences, including the episode where he was nearly carried out in a body bag, and found the physical death to be reaffirming. The journey began, Drury admits, under romantic impressions, he gleaned from a National Geographic documentary. There were times when he questioned why he was subjecting himself to the physical ordeal. He was too stubborn to give up. But just as powerful as his determination was his dedication to the deceased family members he honored with his quest, and the charities, including the Red Cross, St. Jude's, and the Salvation Army that he supported with his hiking.

He got the idea from fellow hikers who, as they shared their experiences, told Drury that he should put his in print. "My memories, experiences, socialization will last a lifetime." He answered with a warm inviting smile and a campfire glow gleaming in his slate-gray eyes. The working title of his book FINDING NORTH will surely inspire others to seek the adventure of their own, perhaps endeavor a journey of the Appalachian Trail.

Not everyone is going to hike the Appalachian Trail. Not everyone wants to, not everyone is able to. But for those who would like to experience the journey vicariously, walking the Trail in Drury's footsteps as they read his words, the book will be a travel guide. Drury's book FINDING NORTH can take you to the Trail, where you'll share the struggles and the triumphs of seven months that Drury, battered in body and exultant in spirit, will always remember.

"Risky" Business

Photos Taken by:
Top: A.T. Conservatory personal.
Bottom Left: "Angie", Bottom Right: "Texas"

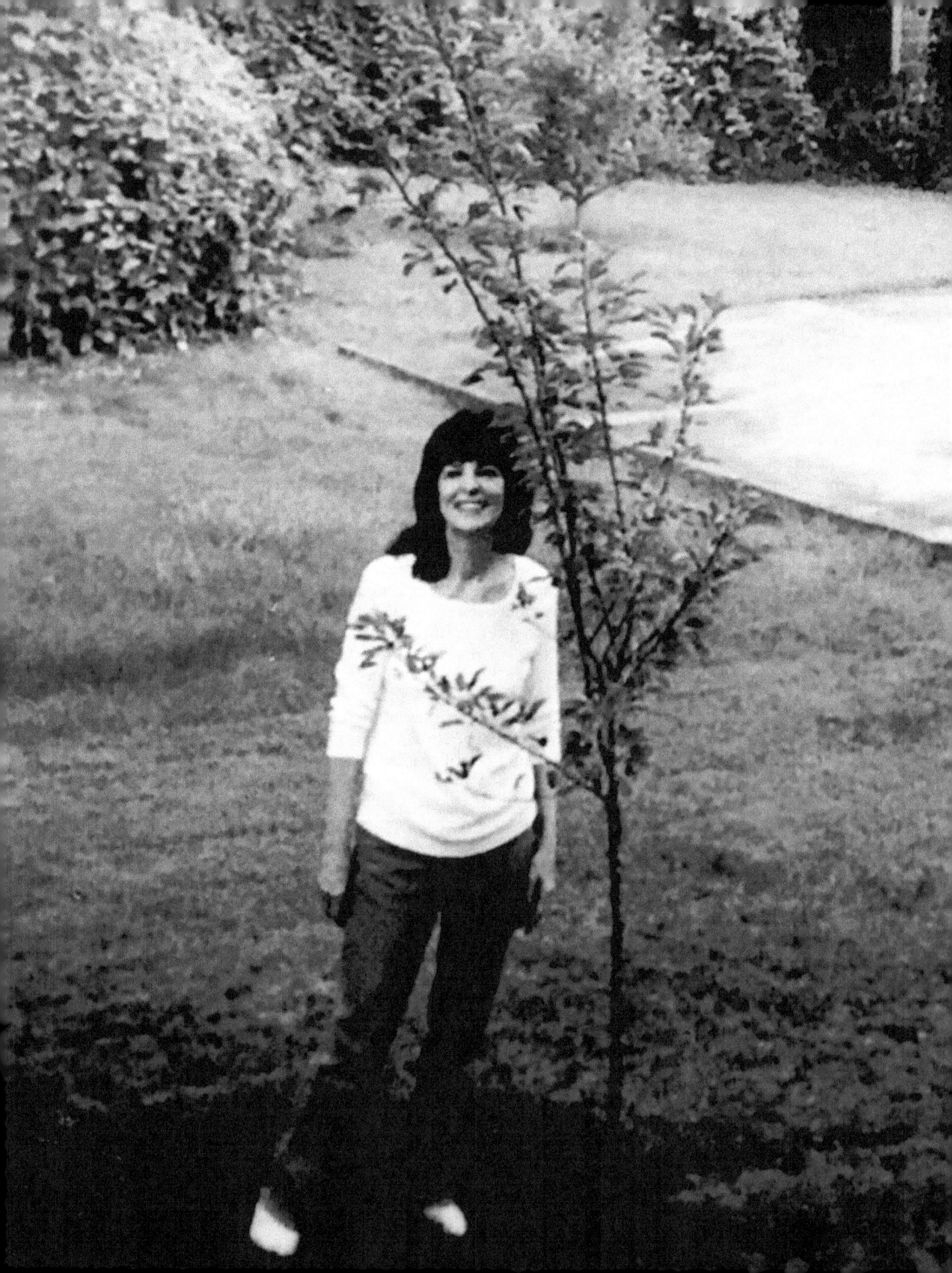

Janet Goven

was born and raised in Pittsburgh, PA, she still resides there with Nick her husband of fifty-seven years. Raising two children, she is now a great-grandmother and she and her husband are both retired. Always an avid reader, her favorite book has been the Bible, which she has read through forty-two times. She loves to teach Bible studies and next to reading and writing, music and singing are her other passions. She also has a deep love for her country and studies its history. Having her work published in many small press magazines across the country down through her twenty years of writing gives her immense pleasure. Westward Quarterly, Pancakes in Heaven, Northern Stars, Ideals, Good Old Days, To God Be The Glory, Bell's Letters, Smile and of course, Gary Drury Publishing©™ Anthologies to name a few.

Excerpt from Tidbits of Poetry & Muse

TIDBITS OF POETRY AND MUSE

What is written here
is from me to you
from days and months
the years, not few
Tidbits of prose
poetry and reason
thoughts of the heart
for every season.

RESCUED

The ground was brown and barren
never dreaming on that day
the snow would soon be falling
and I'd quickly lose my way.
My hopes did melt like liquid
running through my veins as fear
pure panic pranced upon me
I knew my breaking point was near.
A vicious circle I was treading when
a distant bright light did appear
in the darkness I saw the lantern
and someone called "I'm coming, dear".
Down deep relief rolled over me
Replacing my fear and dread
I knew indeed I had been rescued
after all . . . I'm still in bed.

RAGE

Rage rises up within me
yet words cannot be found
so difficult to separate
the thoughts that do abound
As I labor for the strength I need
to comprehend the why
and how you could reject the truth
choose to believe the lie.

The proof was in the giving
how dare you stand there and deny
the evidence, to live was begging
but you chose to let it die
I fought for understanding though
I knew I must retreat
to pen the words of all the ages
and end this pain of gross deceit.

HOMECOMING

Ever so gently, not to disturb
held close to His heart, He carried
with barely a whisper
though convinced I have heard
in that still small voice, He called me.

Ever so gently, the brush in the breath
of His Spirit with mine, he touched me
with barely a heartbeat
though converted, I know
from eternity past, He loved me.

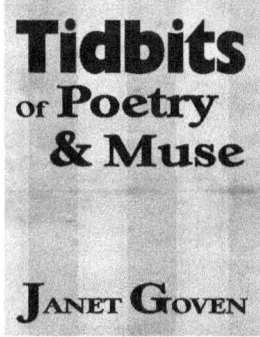 

This is a wonderful collection of poetry and muse. When you just want to set back and relax. Forget about the woes of the world for a few moments. ISBN: 978-1986129237 Page Count: 124 Binding Type: US Trade Paper Trim Size: 9" x 6" Language: English.

ADVENTURES WITH PROVIDENCE

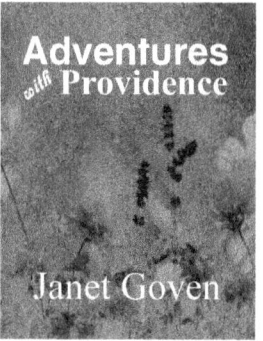

The author shares her collection of fiction and non-fiction stories and her essays and compositions, written with the hope that the reader will enjoy finding peace, hope, goodness, and love as they journey through these adventures. ISBN: 978-1981669806 Page Count: 112 Binding Type: US Trade Paper Trim Size: 8" x 10" Language: English.

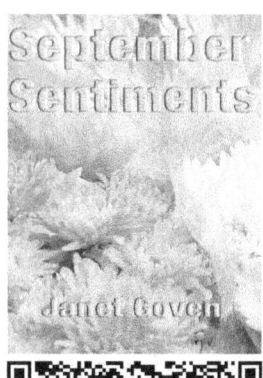

SEPTEMBER SENTIMENTS

Goven wrote this book of fine poetry for her 40th wedding anniversary as a celebration gift for all attendees. Her work clearly demonstrates her grounded philosophies of life. Enjoy these easily relate-able works of arts and share at your next gathering. ISBN: 9781453653913 Page Count: 104 Binding Type: US Trade Paper Trim Size: 8" x 10" Language: English.

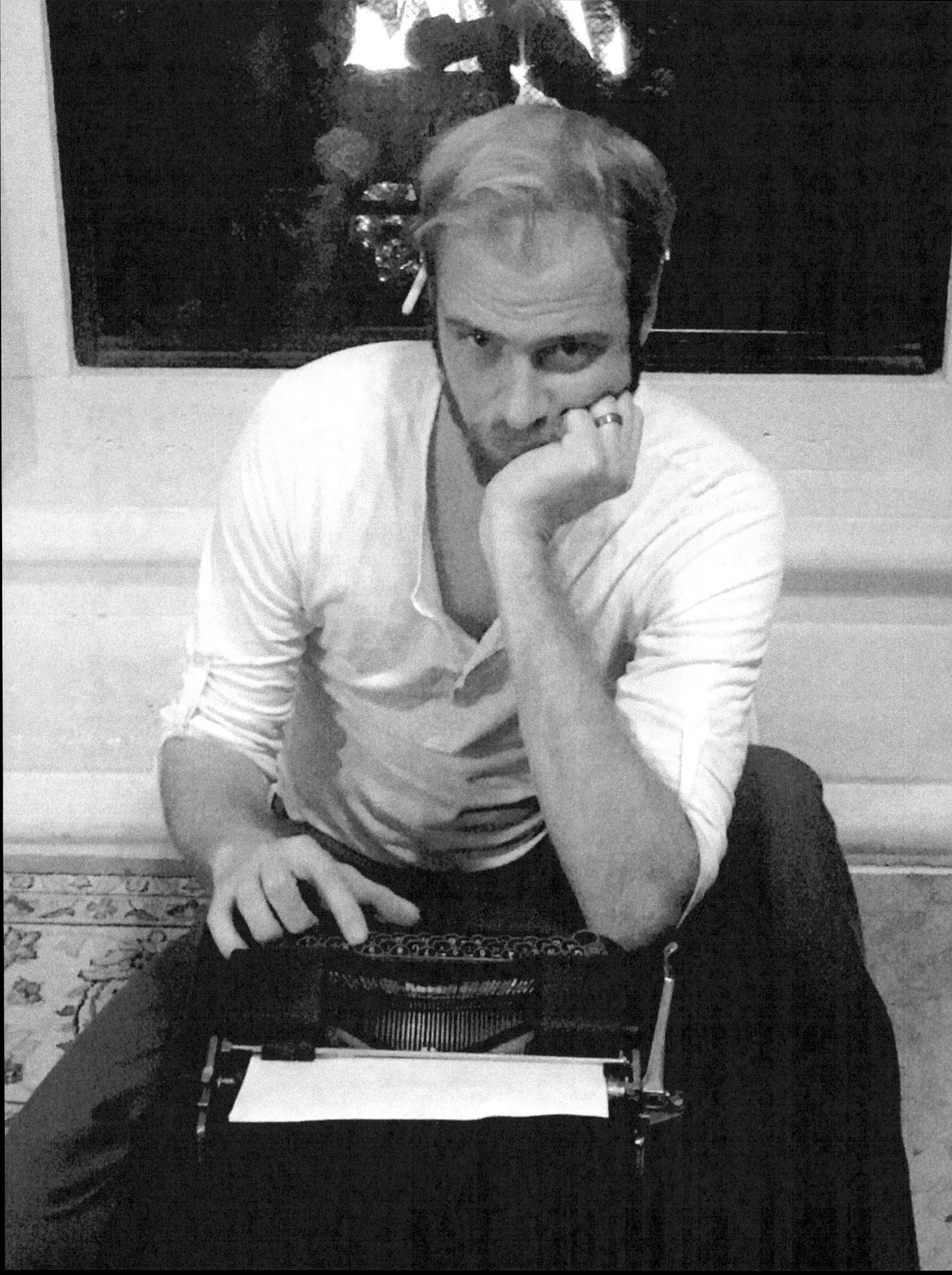

Chris A. Hoppe

is a fiction writer, technical writer, poet, musician, and carpenter who lives in Katy, Texas with his five children and extraordinary wife Monica. He has been writing and spinning tales since the 1990s. His influences include Stephen King, Kurt Vonnegut, Michael Crichton, Ernest Hemingway, and many others.

Excerpt from Hail

Toby had seen the abyss glare at him from the nightmare of the ocean floor, and he had glared back at it, and for that, they had given him a thin-tin medal and put his picture in a fancy book somewhere. Toby wasn't interested in fancy, thin-tin books.

Toby, god bless him, was a weathered soul. His head a pseudo flaxen mess of noodle scrag fighting for survival above a grey and twisted chinmess hanging from a sometimes, but oftentimes, broken jaw; he drank whiskey at sunrise. He swam without suit at twilight, diving deeper, always deeper, until his boat's halogen lights, The Amber's lights, disappeared

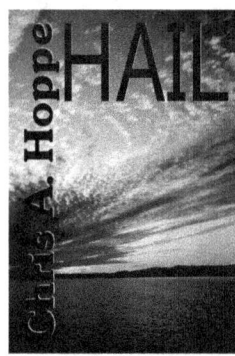 

HAIL is an extended short story about a man lashed with cowardice and the ghosts of his past.

Now, in 2045, the powers that be have brought a seeming savior to our midst, but it freezes the atmosphere, and the atmosphere falls, crushing everything beneath it.

Our "hero," Toby, must find a way to mesh his cowardice with his will to survive, all the while enduring the houndings of his submersible's onboard systems intelligence, LUCI. ISBN: 978-1718760967 Page Count: 44 Binding Type: US Trade Paper Trim Size: 6" x 9" Language: English

completely.

The recordographers had printed their little record book without a quippy anecdote from our champion. Toby had offered, "None of them other nancies even came close", but this had not amused the recordographers. "Show me a more dangerous sport, and I'll show you a bird's nipples."

Such words were not prone to the annuls of sacred record books. Were not? Are not? . . .

#

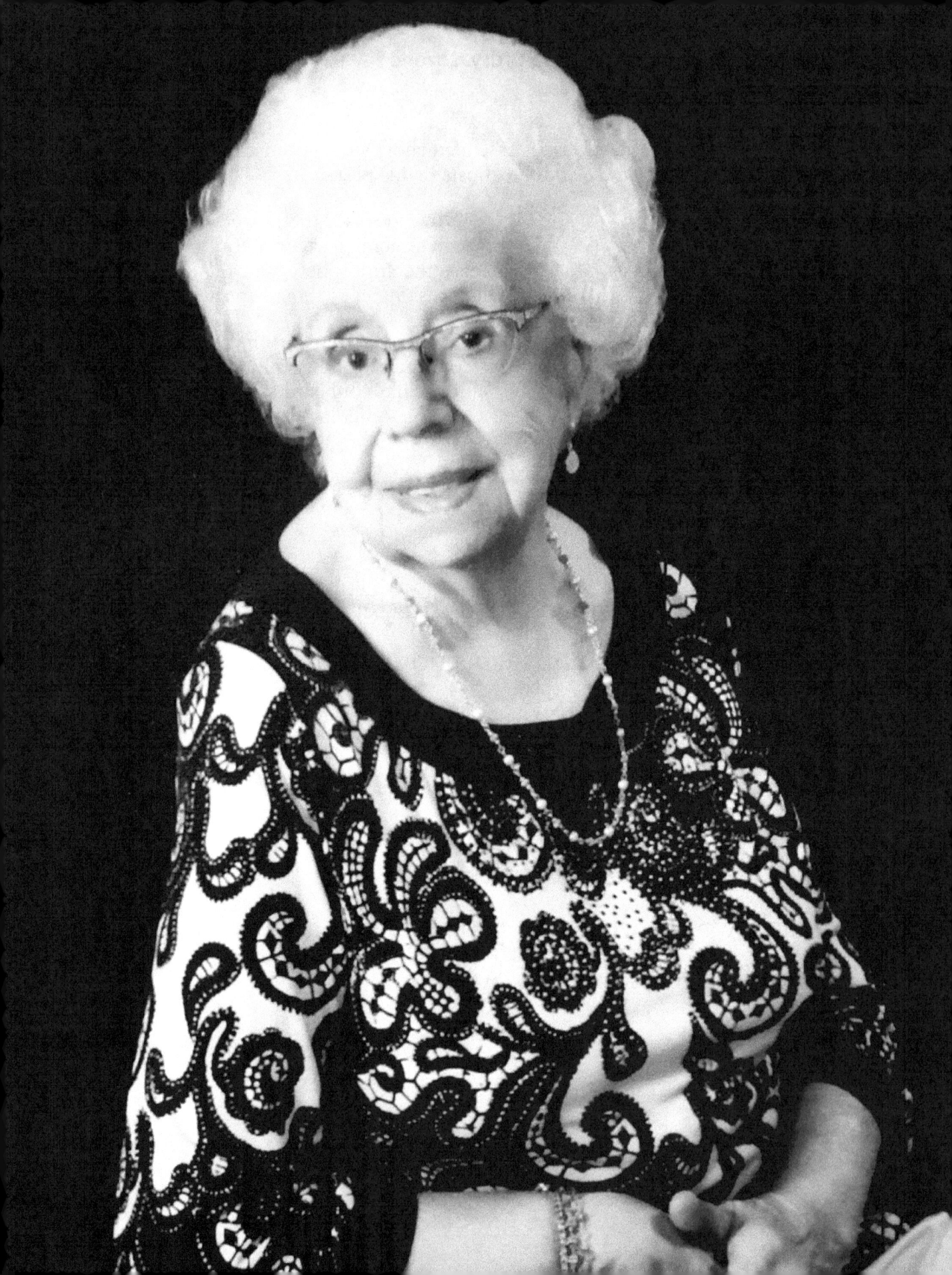

Joyce Johnson

has lived a long life, having been born in North Dakota in 1918. She has survived two World Wars and the big Depression as well as minor wars and recessions. She was the first daughter of my parents after four husky sons. Her brothers dearly loved having a baby sister. Johnson left North Dakota in July of 1941 and went to Detroit, Michigan where her betrothed had gone to find work. They left there in February of 1943 in order to be near her family which had moved to Washington State. Johnson's son was born two weeks after they got here. She has lived in the beautiful Skagit Valley in Washington ever since to eventually raise family, her son and two daughters. Meanwhile, in 1962 after 21 years of marriage, her husband had died suddenly and she had been left to fend for herself and children.

Excerpts from Lifetime Memories in Verse

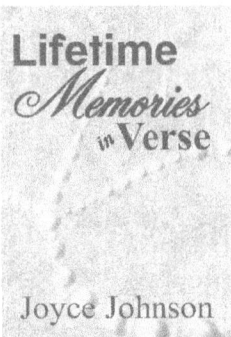

LIFETIME MEMORIES IN VERSE

book of poetry is made up of rhymes and thoughts that I have written down in the last twenty years of my life. They are memories of my early life and laments about my advanced age and a bit about my surroundings and my family. I have written about flowers and nature but those have been published in another resource so I have not included an excess of them here. Please read and enjoy. I was eighty years old before I wrote a single one of them. ISBN: 978-1981640768 Page Count: 158 Binding Type: US Trade Paper Trim Size: 6" x 9" Language: English

From my Point View

I wouldn't be so irritated
As I am when I find you
Have opened the door and walked right in,
If you would just shut it behind you!

A dog's life is really easy,
You needn't pay the monthly rent
Or worry about high prices.
With small things you are content.

I'm always at your beck and call.
You want in, then you want out.
You don't worry about escaping heat
And then wonder why I shout.

The first of April hasn't brought
The warmth of Spring this year.,
So we must both conserve a bit
Since fuel oil is so dear.

I know that all my fussing
Is falling on deaf ears
But life for me is not as soft
As in your eyes it appears.

The sun is shining brightly
And the grass is greening too
But Susie, I can't come out to play.
It's only thirty-two. (Fahrenheit that is.)

Thankfulness

The day has dawned both bright and clear
    With lovely November weather
Another Thanksgiving day has come
    When we can be together.

We're thankful for the blessings
    That have been ours this year
And pray for the protection
    Of all those we hold most dear.

We remember the hungry of the world
    The homeless and the ill
And ask your blessing on them too
    If this should be thy will.
        Amen

Letter to Santa

Dear Santa. I fear I've not always been good
Nor minded my mama as much as I should.
But I didn't mean it and if you will come
I'll leave you some cookies, some milk and some gum.

I pulled the cat's tail till he jumped and meowed,
And scratched my dear daddy who hollered aloud.
He said I would find an old rock in my sock,
But Mama said, "Hush, you're reacting to shock."

She suggested that I should just write you to say,
I'm sorry and I will try hard to obey.
I love you, dear Santa and if you forgive,
I'll carry the trash out each day that I live.

Don't listen to Sister who can't take a joke.
Could you bring her a doll for the one that I broke?
Tell my daddy you think I should have one more chance
And not do as he threatened to send me to France.

Daddy's Table

Just a little library table
Always in our living room.
With the bible that lay on it
It became a loved heirloom.

Grandma bought it for my daddy
Just to make his home less bare
When she visited Dakota
And his little homestead there.

Daddy loved that little table
And presented it with pride
To my mama when he married
His beloved and cherished bride.

Mama took care of that table,
Rubbed it to a lovely glow,
Giving it the place of honor
Because she loved my daddy so.

When our home was lost to fire
He made sure we were alive
Then rushed in to save the table
In the year of thirty-five.

Daddy died and then my mama
But the table still remains,
Relic of those days in history;
Homesteading on Dakota plains.

Cost a pittance when she bought it
In the year nineteen ought two
She'd be surprised at how we prize it,
If our grandma only knew.

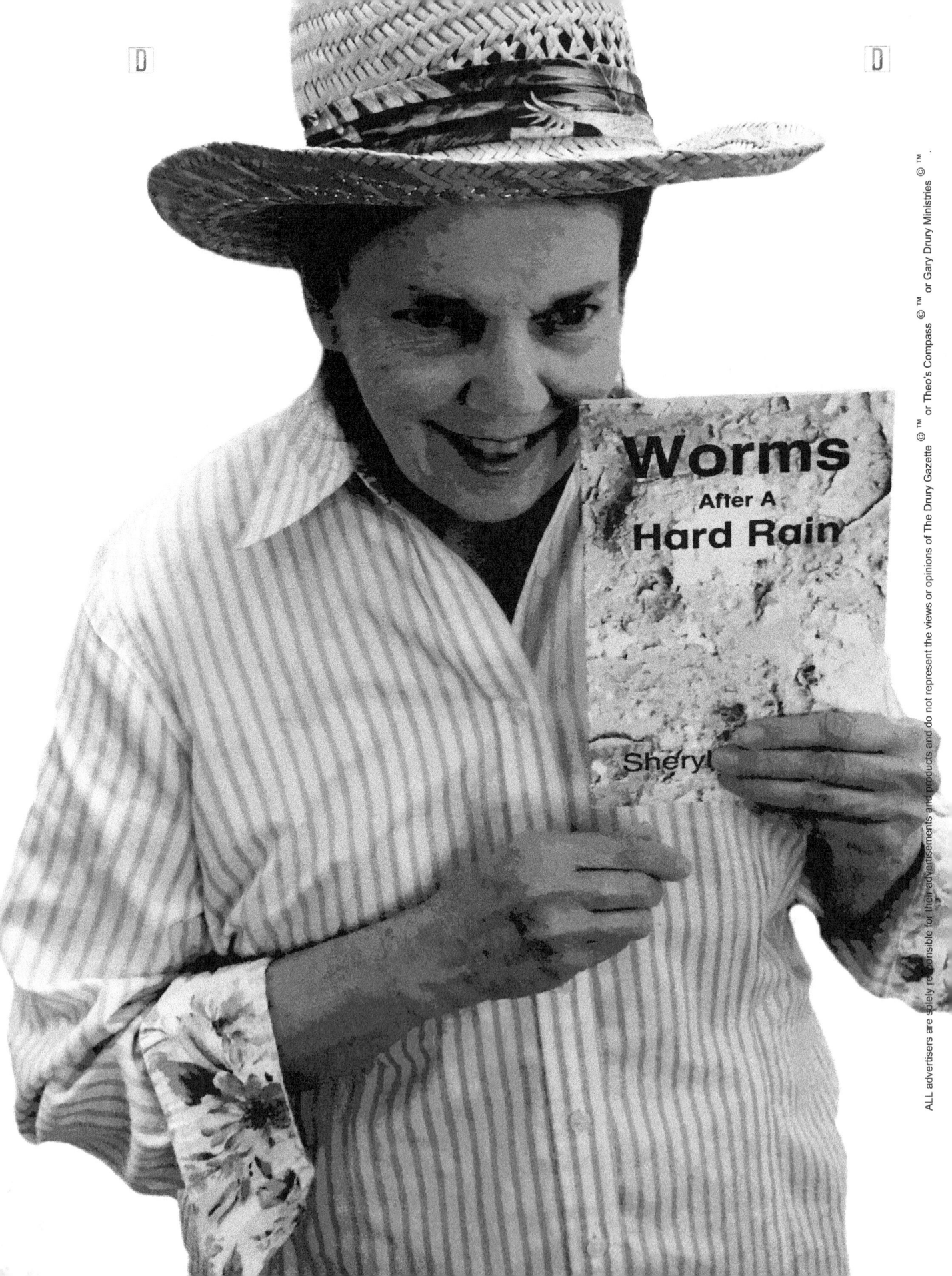

Sheryl L. Nelms

was the Editor of Oakwood, the SDSU literary magazine. She was a Contributing Editor to Byline, a national writers' magazine and to Streets, a national literary magazine. She was the Editor of Crawford's Chronicles, an insurance trade publication. She's been a Staff Writer for several newspapers and magazines. She's currently the Fiction/Nonfiction editor of The Pen Woman Magazine, the national membership magazine of the National League of American Pen Women, a Contributing Editor for Time of Singing, A Magazine of Christian Poetry and a four-time Pushcart Prize nominee. Sheryl is a member of the National League of American Pen Women, The Society of Southwestern Authors, Abilene Writer's Guild and Trinity Writers Workshop. She's also an insurance agent, a painter, a weaver, and an old dirt biker.

No Hats or Bib Overalls On Dance Night

is a collection of poetry about people. The sections are Street People, Working Folks, A Bubble That's Slightly Off Center and The Smorgasbord. This book includes poems about bag ladies, bums and panhandlers. There are cremated ashes, a packing plant gut shoveler, an armed robber, a pre-planned funeral party, a cross-dressing trucker, a dentist, a cowboy, the Copper Queen, and a bootlegger. These categories cover the spectrum of life. From sad to happy to belly laughing funny. It is a book of unconditional poetry! ISBN: 978-1986319225

Worms After A Hard Rain

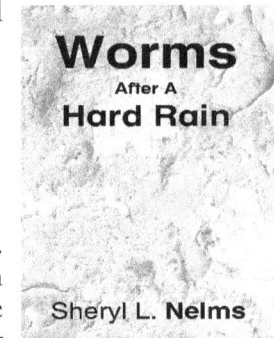

is the title of my seventy-one poem manuscript. This manuscript won the Schultz-Werth Research Award at South Dakota State University and five hundred dollars. This book is an account of my life. It chronicles some of the things I've seen and done from hog slopping to visiting the Amon Carter Art Museum. From the Milwaukee zoo to a thunderstorm in Pinetop, Arizona. It contains bits of historical fact and fiction. I take you along across the United States. I transport the reader with me back to the 1950s for a gentle summer day. We go on a tour of the Cudahy Packing Plant, coyote hunting, pheasant hunting, grave digging and taking out the trash. We survive a train wreck, a flying saucer, and a South Dakota blizzard. Through it, all the writing prevails. ISBN: 978-1981523375

The Stalking Spirits

a book of nitty-gritty poetry. From the "Grey Sidewalk Man" to the "The Copper Queen," the people in this collection are hanging on tight. The scenery shifts from Texas to Arizona to New Mexico to Kansas to Illinois and to Canada. The subjects vary from drunk rolling to picking gooseberries, to box turtles. All reminding us of The Grand Masterflash's song "The Message" when it says, "Don't push me cause I'm close to the edge!" We too slip when that "West Texas Preacher" slides in the mud down into the hole at the graveside service he is preaching in the rain. We feel the bewilderment when the ER nurse asked us to move our feet and we've been sitting so long that we can't feel them, don't know where they are. Through it all, the words take us there and bring us back ISBN: 978-1981523467

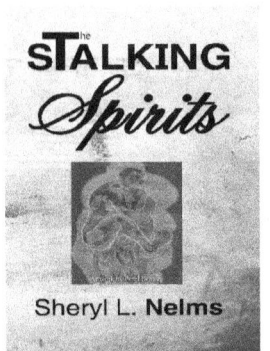

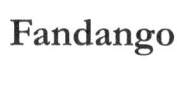

Fandango

I hunch behind him
on the express
bus

watch
two oriental
cockroaches

trot to
and fro

across his rumpled
white collar

then up into
his greasy
brown hair

back down
his neck

until he
brushes them
off

— © Sheryl Nelms

Frogs

the dark
and the rain
brought them out

hopping across Highway 15

until the cars
hit them

popping them
Like

boiling cranberries

— © Sheryl Nelms

South Dakota Spring

great cracks
and groans

rasp across the Big Sioux River

pressure ridges
Rise

swoop into
Synclines

pushed down from North Dakota

melt holes
materialize midstream

where the current
gnaws away

at winter's
Iced

cinch

— © Sheryl Nelms

Steve Nottingham

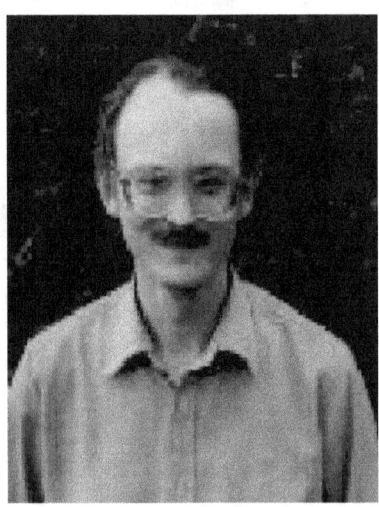

"Nasansa Endures" is a result of Steve Nottingham's lifelong interest in lost world stories, everything from Conan Doyle's classic "The Lost World" to the recent sequel "Dinosaur Summer" by Michael Crichton and the latter's two Jurassic Park novels, which became block-busting movies. Nottingham is also a great admirer of the works Rider Haggard and Edgar Rice Burroughs, who wrote many fascinating lost world novels of their own. In addition, Steve Nottingham has a great interest in factual books on dinosaurs and paleontology. He's also interested in Africa; not so much the Africa of today but the mysterious Dark Continent of yesteryear. He's particularly fascinated by accounts of those courageous white explorers who first penetrated Africa's wilds at great risk to their own lives. Nasansa Endures (Nasansa is the name of Nottingham's own lost world) he's interested in all elements have come together, and he had great pleasure in chronicling this fictional adventure.

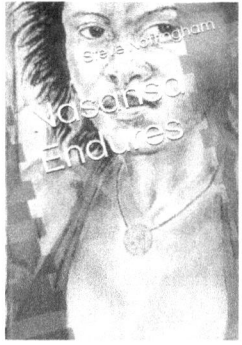 

Nasasna Endures

"Nasansa Endures" is a result of Steve Nottingham's lifelong interest in lost world stories, everything from Conan Doyle's classic "The Lost World" to the recent sequel "Dinosaur Summer" by Michael Crichton and the latter's two Jurassic Park novels, which became blockbusting movies. Nottingham is also a great admirer of the works Rider Haggard and Edgar Rice Burroughs, who wrote many fascinating lost world novels of their own. In addition, Steve Nottingham has a great interest in factual books on dinosaurs and paleontology. He's also interested in Africa; not so much the Africa of today but the mysterious Dark Continent of yesteryear. He's particularly fascinated by accounts of those courageous white explorers who first penetrated Africa's wilds at great risk to their own lives. Nasansa Endures (Nasansa is the name of Nottingham's own lost world) he's interested in all elements have come together, and he had great pleasure in chronicling this fictional adventure. ISBN-13: 978-1520473857 Page Count: 172 Binding Type: US Trade Paper Trim Size: 6" x 9" Language: English

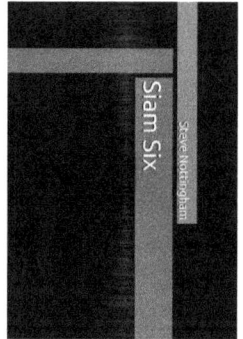 

Siam Six

This action-packed adventure novel backdropped in Thailand about a special team formed of six people from myriad military service backgrounds are known as The Siam Six. Their covert operation's purpose is to combat unique threats and crises which can't be dealt with by Thailand's conventional armed forces. The Siam Six stealth forces soon find themselves facing dangers which test their special abilities to the limit. Their wide-ranging missions take them from the bustling overcrowded sprawl of Bangkok into the jungles of Cambodia and then the ocean depths off southern Thailand. ISBN-13: 978-1520468952 Page Count: 190 Binding Type: US Trade Paper Trim Size: 6" x 9" Language: English

Excerpt from Nasansa Endures

Being careful to avoid all towns and villages, Haines and Masina followed the winding course of the Gambia further inland. Most of the time they were out of sight of the river, not wanting to risk being spotted by those traversing the Gambia aboard the many craft which plied its muddy waters. The two fugitives sustained themselves by living off the land. Fortunately for Haines, Masina knew what was safe to eat and what wasn't. They staved off their hunger pangs by eating such things as the fruit of shea trees and the edible pods of nita trees. There was still no sign of any pursuit after several days, and by then Haines and Masina realized that perhaps it wasn't so strange that they hadn't been apprehended. After all, this was Africa, not England, and they weren't likely to run into a policeman or the like on the banks of the Gambia.

In truth there was no real law enforcement at all, at least not that of the white man. Of course, Edmundson's death would have been reported to Jonkakonda's alkaid by now, the African equivalent of a head magistrate. However, there was little the alkaid could do even though he must know that the vanished Haines and Masina were responsible for the Englishman's death. The alkaid had neither the men or resources to search for the pair. Even if he'd had an army of searchers, tracking down two people in these wilds would have been like searching for a needle in a haystack. All that the alkaid could do was advise the nearest towns and villages to be on the lookout for Haines and Masina. Masina had decided that their best course of action would be to lie low for a while and slowly begin to work their way to her home town of Wawra near Banbera. Once they reached her family, they would take them in and hide them until all of the fuss died down. Not having a better plan, Haines agreed to this. So it was that they gradually began to work their way toward distant Wawra. It would take them some months to reach Masina's home town. In a way Haines was glad of this, for it gave him ample time to get to know Masina better. He felt drawn to her in a way that he never had any woman before - white or black. Nor was it just a matter of physical attraction, for he also admired Masina's courage and intelligence and the increasing glimpses he was seeing of her kindness and affection. Haines guessed that at heart Masina was a loving and affectionate woman, but that she had learnt to mask these traits due to the terrible rigors which she'd passed through since her abduction by the Slateens. The ordeal of the long march had left its mark on the lovely African in this way and others.

Excerpt from Siam Six

Don Muang Air Force Base, Bangkok Outside, bright sunlight beat down on tarmaced runways and an F-15 taxing onto an active runway for take-off. The loud thrumming of the Air Force jet's engines was clearly audible, while overhead another jet arced through the blue, cloudless sky with a howling, reverberating boom. Sealed away from these sights and sounds, four men now sat around a table in the briefing room of the airfield's 12-B Building. Here there was silence save for low, murmured voices and the background whisper of the air-conditioning system. Seated at the head of the table was General Narai; a short but burly Thai officer with broad shoulders and a thickening waist. Save for a few stray wisps of greying hair, he was almost completely bald, and he wore wire spectacles. The other three men were also top-ranking military officers; two of them were Air Force men like Narai, and the third was an army colonel. Calling this meeting to order, Narai now spoke up, "Gentlemen, let's get down to business. As you know, this meeting has been arranged to brief you on Project Siam Six, a project which is both top secret and very important to Thailand's future defense. "For some time now we've been aware of the need for a small but effective fighting force to supplement our existing armed forces. The recent terrorist activities of the Al-Quaeda in America — the attack on the Pentagon and the destruction of the Twin Towers — has made it even more clear that we need an adequate defense and deterrent against such activities. "For this reason and others. Project Siam Six has been instituted. Our plan is to assemble and train six people drawn from our armed forces who will function as a team to handle those situations which our conventional forces can't effectively deal with. "At present we are still in the process of selecting possible candidates for the Siam Six team by going through our records of Air Force and Army personnel." At this point one of the Air Force officers cleared his throat and gained Narai's attention. "Excuse me. General, but isn't that somewhat irregular? Can we not find our candidates among the Air Force without having to look elsewhere?" "Yes, it is somewhat unusual. General Chavalit, but our only concern is with finding the best people for Siam Six, and it's unimportant whether they come from the Air Force or Army. "We're also in the process of purchasing a special helicopter for our team — one which will give our people rapid transport and a good weapons system. We've decided on a Nighthawk helicopter, and it's due to be shipped to us from America within several days."

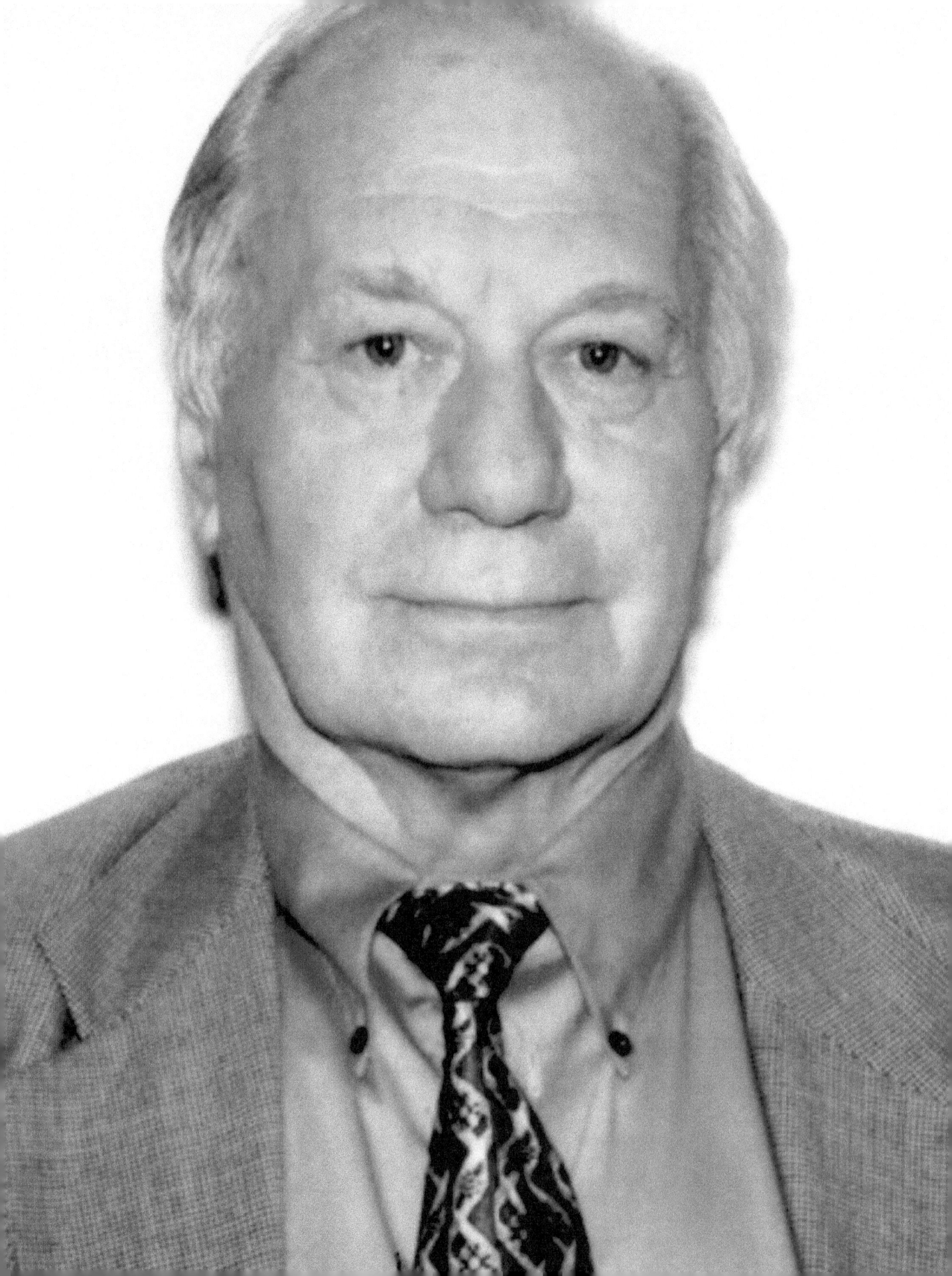

Adolf P. Shvedchikov

is a romantic poet. He is the master of love lyrics. But for him, love lyrics are not an independent goal. He tries to understand the whole spectrum of relationships between a man and a woman, to find the secret of a harmonic world in the categories of love. A great place in the poet's work is the theme of the relationship between a person and the world around him. He tries to find the philosophical meaning of life and wants to understand what human capabilities are in a relatively short time of his existence. I want to believe that this book can be of interest to the English-speaking and Russian-speaking readers.

Adolf Shvedchikov novella **FELLOW FROM DONBASS** telling about the difficult post-war years of childhood and youth of Andrew Arbenin, who lives in one of the mines settlements of Donbass. The story tells his fate of almost half a century of his life from 1944 to 1990. After graduating from school, he succeeds in entering Moscow State University. Later becoming a research fellow of one of the leading research institutes of the USSR Academy of Sciences in Moscow. Shvedchikov story is devoted to his hero's family drama. Many interesting details and his perspective of that difficult era in the Soviet Union. Which for the modern generation has become a frightfully long distant history. ISBN: 978-1987732610 Page Count: 170 Binding Type: US Trade Paper Trim Size: 6" x 9" Language: English

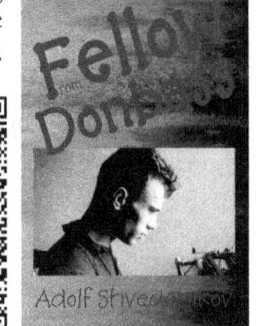

AGAIN, THE POPLARS SPREAD THEIR BITTER SCENT

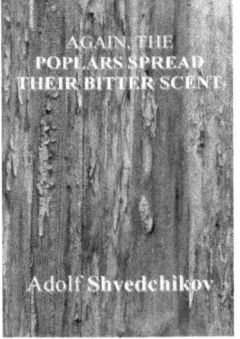

is a delightful book of poetry. Over the past 20 years, his poetic work became well known in Russia and abroad thanks to numerous publications. His poems systematically appear in various Anthologies and are published in the journals New Literature (Russia), Libelle (France), Pluma y tintero (Spain), Episteme, Our Poetry Archive (India), The World Poets Quarterly (China). Recently in Germany were published 5 books of his poetry: Jungle of Love, Crooked Mirrors of Imagination, Unknown eternal chains, the time has come, to sum up, River of Life. Adolf Shvedchikov is a romantic poet. He is the master of love lyrics. But for him, love lyrics are not an independent goal. ISBN: 978-1984985507 Page Count: 60 Binding Type: US Trade Paper Trim Size: 6" x 9" Language: English

Over 150 Romanticized **WILLIAM SHAKESPEARE SONNETS** are now translated into Russian thanks to Dr. Adolf Pavlovich Shvedchikov Russian scientist, poet, and translator. The William Shakespeare SONNETS translated in Russian is the perfect companion for students, teachers, colleges, universities or anyone studying the exquisite Russian language. English/Russian Version: ISBN: 978-1985131163 Page Count: 172 Binding Type: US Trade Paper Trim Size: 6" x 9" Language: English & Russian

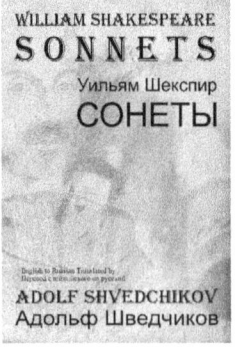

TEARS OF BLISS Readers are given the opportunity to see the collection of poems "Tears of Bliss" by the famous Russian scientist, poet, and translator Adolf Pavlovich Shvedchikov, whose work is well known all over the world. His poems, translated into many languages, are printed in various countries in journals and anthologies. Be the flame of my soul; The world is beating convulsively." Over the past 20 years, he gained fame not only in Russia but in many countries around the world. His poems are regularly published in international literary journals and anthologies, he is a member of various international literary societies. His books of poetry were printed in many countries (Russia, USA, Germany, Japan, Cyprus). Adolf Shvedchikov - the master of love lyrics, in his poems he constantly sings the female beauty. We hope that the book "Tears of Bliss" can be of interest to the English and Russian-speaking readers in different countries. ISBN: 978-1985378773 Page Count: 106 Binding Type: US Trade Paper Trim Size: 6" x 9" Language: English

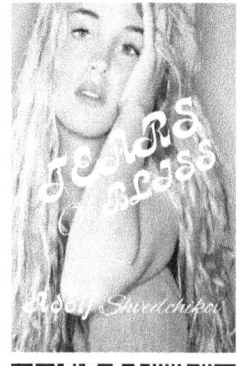

AGAIN, THE POPLARS SPREAD THEIR BITTER SCENT is a delightful book of poetry. Over the past 20 years, his poetic work became well known in Russia and abroad thanks to numerous publications. His poems systematically appear in various Anthologies and are published in the journals New Literature (Russia), Libelle (France), Pluma y tintero (Spain), Episteme, Our Poetry Archive (India), The World Poets Quarterly (China). Recently in Germany were published 5 books of his poetry: Jungle of Love, Crooked Mirrors of Imagination, Unknown eternal chains, the time has come, to sum up, River of Life. Adolf Shvedchikov is a romantic poet. He is the master of love lyrics. But for him, love lyrics are not an independent goal. ISBN: 978-1981518135 Page Count: 110 Binding Type: US Trade Paper Trim Size: 6" x 9" Language: English & Russian

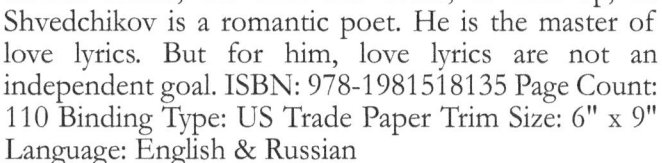

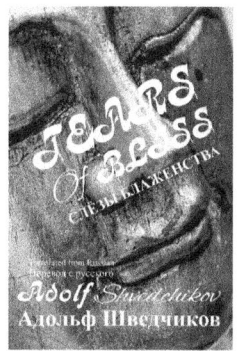

TEARS OF BLISS Readers are given the opportunity to see the collection of poems "Tears of Bliss" by the famous Russian scientist, poet, and translator Adolf Shvedchikov. His poems, translated into many languages, are printed in various countries in journals and anthologies. Be the flame of my soul; The world is beating convulsively." Over the past 20 years, he gained fame not only in Russia but in many countries around the world. His poems are regularly published in international literary journals and anthologies, he is a member of various international literary societies.

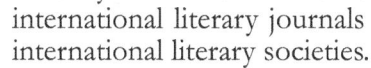

His books of poetry were printed in many countries (Russia, USA, Germany, Japan, Cyprus). Adolf Shvedchikov - the master of love lyrics, in his poems he constantly sings the female beauty. We hope that the book "Tears of Bliss" can be of interest to the English and Russian-speaking readers in different countries. ISBN: 978-1985378056 Page Count: 118 Binding Type: US Trade Paper Trim Size: 6" x 9" Language: English & Russian

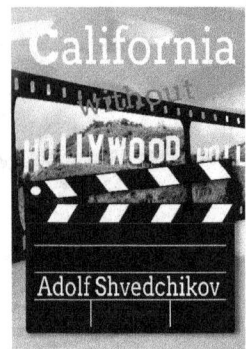

Born in Donbass (the town Shakhty, Russia) in a family of miners. My childhood and adolescence took place in a difficult time after World War II in one small mining settlement. I first met California, thanks to Hollywood films with Charlie Chaplin, who was very popular at that time in the USSR. Especially remembered the film "City Lights". The musical comedy "Sun Valley Serenade" with the Glenn Miller Orchestra and the famous Chattanooga Choo Choo melody was also very popular. Later in my youth, I read books by American writers: Jack London, Mark Twain, Ernest Hemingway, John Steinbeck, poets Emilia Dickinson, Walt Whitman, who told about life in an unknown country of America.

California Without Hollywood ISBN: 978-1796917758 Page Count: 46 Binding Type: US Trade Paper Trim Size: 6" x 9" Language: English

Since childhood, two elements have struggled in me: an interest in the exact sciences and a passion for literary creativity. This is not surprising, because the Russian people were brought up on the books of such excellent writers as L.N. Tolstoy, F.I. Dostoevsky, N.V. Gogol, A.P. Chekhov and the poets A.S. Pushkin, M. Yu. Lermontov, Anna Akhmatova, Alexander Blok, Boris Pasternak, and others. Therefore, it is not surprising that in the '60s-'70s of the twentieth century, among the technical intelligentsia, there were eternal disputes between "physicists" and "lyricists". Passion for Russian literature is one of the most common among Russians. I was no exception. I began to write my first poems in early childhood. But then after graduating from high school, I entered the Moscow State University and the exact sciences became my profession. After graduating from university, I worked for many years at one of the leading institutions of the Academy of Sciences of the USSR. But poetry has always been my hobby. I wanted my work to be known not only in Russia but also in other countries.

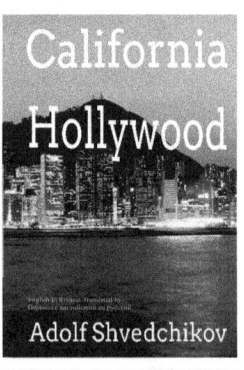

California Without Hollywood ISBN: 978-1796824483 Page Count: 74 Binding Type: US Trade Paper Trim Size: 6" x 9" Language: English & Russian

Therefore, I began to study English more thoroughly, so that readers could familiarize themselves with my work in translation. In the late 90s and early 2000s, I began to publish abroad in various poetic journals and anthologies. I was able to visit the USA for the first time in 1993. I have been to many American cities (New York, Washington, San Francisco, Los Angeles, Santa Barbara, Las Vegas, Salt Lake City), but most of all I liked

California. Upon returning to Moscow, I published my first book, "My Discovery of America." After that, I repeatedly visited Los Angeles and became increasingly acquainted with the life of this state not only as a world center of the film industry. I tried to express my impressions of California without Hollywood in a poetic form in the proposed collection of poems. Such verses as California, the Pacific sunset, Palm Springs, Encino, Oh, time, you are like the Pacific Ocean, Eternal sleep is near and dear to me. I would like my readers to see California, not through the eyes of a tourist, but to feel the specificity of this unusual US state with a poetic feeling.

Excerpts from Fellow from Donbass

It was a hard time, and Andrew was lucky to some extent that they were able to find shelter with Veronika in Zinaida Fyodorovna's house. Heavy everyday life was compensated to some extent by the fact Zinaida Fedorovna brought home something from the remnants of children's cuisine. Manna or millet porridge, dried fruit compote, and sometimes even a glass of milk! Life was gradually entering a new direction. Veronica issued bread and food cards, no longer starved to death. Veronica went to work early in the morning. Sometimes she had to go all the way, all ten kilometers. But usually she was picked up on the road by truck drivers who were transporting coal to the railway station. Work at the mine was very hard, there was still a war, men were sorely lacking, there were many women who manually transported the trolleys with coal. Techniques were practically non-existent, the miners worked in the old manner with a hack and a hammer with a sharp tip at the end, sometimes in a lying position, since the coal seams in Donbass usually did not exceed one meter. They descended into the mine and ascended to the surface along the stairs, sometimes several hundred meters. Veronica was planning the mine workings.

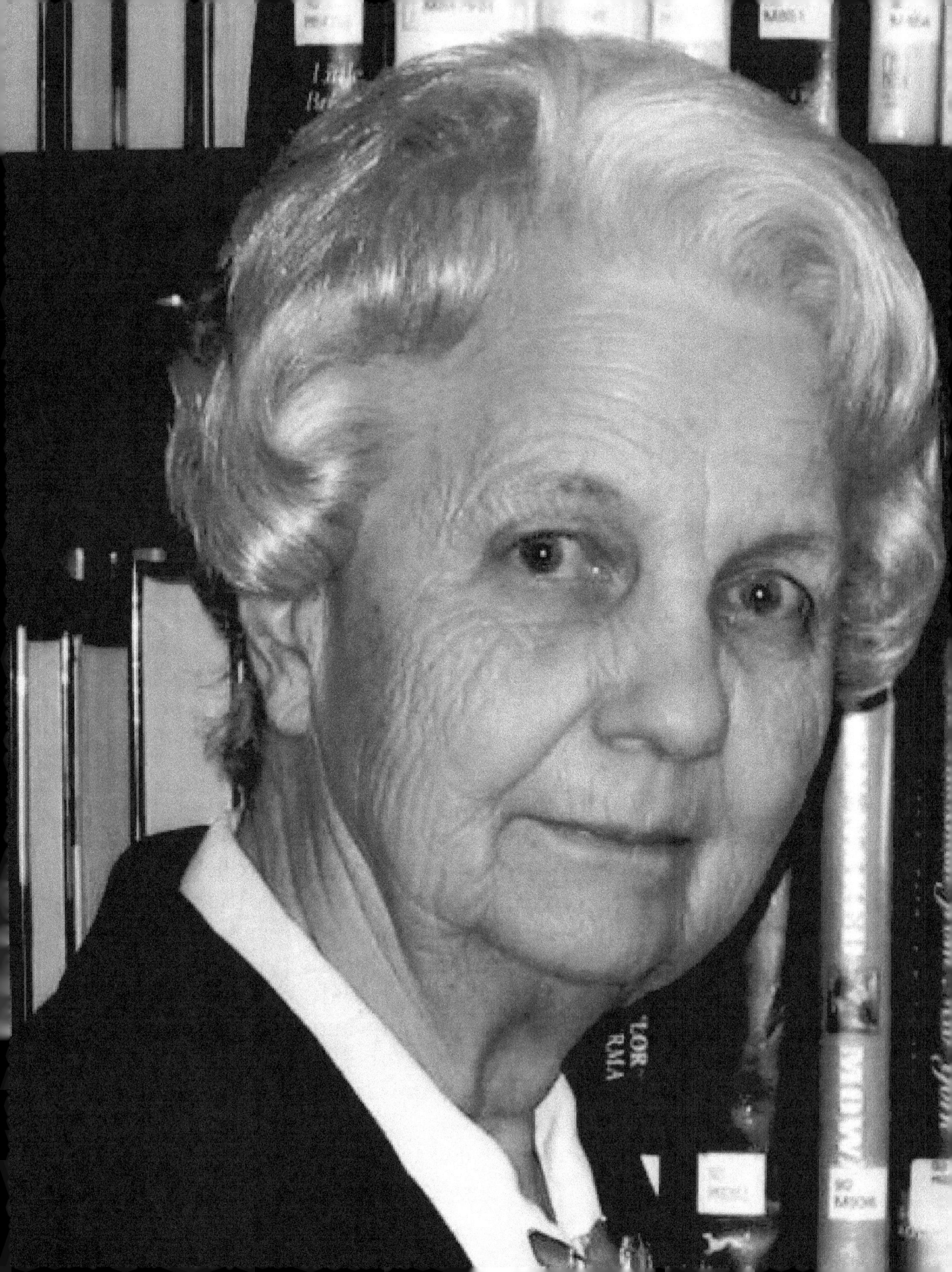

Marion H. Youngquist

was born and educated in Salem. Oregon. She's written for newspapers, magazines, and served as a church editor. She's also won prizes for her poems and plays. Her four books Procula, Maple Tree Tales, The Rocky Road Year, and Christmas Presence were released earlier by Gary Drury Publishing©™. Her advice: Write in spite of a good excuse.

Procula

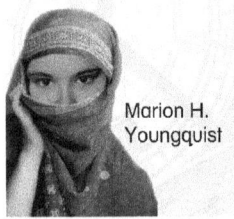

Procula, a young girl, raised by wealthy relatives in Rome. Years later marries Pontius Pilate, an Army officer, who is sent to Palestine as Emperor Tiberius' personal representative. When Jesus is jailed, Procula warns Pilate. Ignoring Procula. Pilate is summoned to Rome. Somehow Procula manages their escape. This adventure story, based on a plethora of years of historical research, recreates Procula a lesser known Biblical personality. Throughout history, she is only mentioned briefly three times. What power did she hold, if any? One woman's (Marion H. Youngquist) childhood quest has brought her to this conclusion-- After her own history-making ordeal in New York City on Tuesday morning September 11, 2001. PROCULA novel sports a wealth of researched historical facts intertwined with deception, Intrigue, and mystery surrounding Pontius Pilate's and wife PROCULA. Procula is a strong independent self-awarded woman that is clearly prevalent in this novel of a young ubiquitous girl. Whom one day may have held the power to alter the course of history. Women throughout the world will easily relate to Procula's rise and potential fall. ISBN-13: 978-0692747391 Pages: 166 Type: US Trade Paper Trim Size: 9" x 6" Language: English

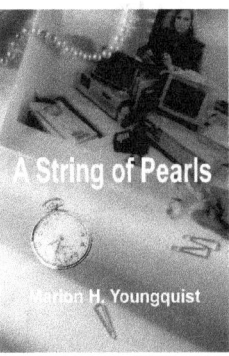

A String of Pearls

On December 7, 1941 (Pearl Harbor Day), the lives of Anna Marie Schulz and her classmates are forever changed. In her four years at McNaughton College during World War II, Anna Marie experiences to humor and heartache as her boyfriends leave, die or return. This novel is a tribute to Anna Marie's own struggles and that of "the greatest generation" with their ultimate victory. In book clubs, many memories are shared of war years. One morning a phantom character, a little girl who lived during the Depression, came into my consciousness. She said that her name was Anna Marie Schultz. She commanded me to Write my story. I knew nothing more about her. Two outlined novels were set aside because Anna Marie demanded my attention. Quickly, her story became larger and deeper than I could have anticipated. She placed herself as eight, going on nine in 1932, during the Great Depression. I remember it well. ISBN-13: 978-1453716816 Pages: 302 Type: US Trade Paper Trim Size: 9" x 6" Language: English

Excerpt from Procula

On my first morning, an older woman awakened me. She was thin with prominent hard muscles on her slim arms. Blue veins webbed her agile hands. Her gray hair was in a twisted bun. In all, she appeared neat and tidy, but a conspicuous hump on her back was obvious. However, her eyes were kind and the hazel glints in them added to her unusual appearance. She carried a tray with fruit and bread, and a glass of milk.

"I'm called Weaver. Eat up, and wash yourself clean before we go to your aunt." She handed me a soft towel – perhaps the softest I'd ever felt – and turned to leave the room. "Be sure to wear clean clothing."

I ate slowly, amused that Weaver would tell me what to wear. Did this household in Roma think I was so ignorant that I wouldn't be clean and properly dressed?

It was late in the morning before we went to Zia Terentia. Her personal slave was fixing Zia Terentia's black hair in the Grecian style of curls around her face with a knot crowning her head. A silver mirror and inlaid ivory combs were beside a tray of glittering rings. Several were heavy gold, set with sparkling stones. One was coiled like a tiny snake with emerald pinpoint eyes. My aunt was intent, choosing a ring for every finger. She took them on and off. She lifted her hand and waved each ring to catch the light. She considered every one carefully. It was like a choreographed dance. I was fascinated by her quick frowns and quicker smile over each choice. Carefully, her slave painted my aunt's lips and lined her eyes. With arched eyebrows, Zia Terentia began her instructions as she sipped a goblet of red wine.

"Procula, you must realize that I'm extremely busy. The demands upon my time are endless." She gave a deep sigh. "Already this morning, Lucius has dealt with the hawkers beyond the courtyard. They wish to sell us rugs ... perfumes ... nuts ... only the finest things. Roman merchants want our business. They love to sell to this household. Then I must approve all of Lucius' decisions." She gave me a stern look. "You will realize, as you get older, how important this address is. You're very fortunate to live here."

I lowered my eyes and hoped that I nodded humbly enough. I looked at Weaver, bent and impassive. Our eyes were almost at the same level.

Zia Terentia rattled on, ". . . I am placing you under the direction of Weaver here. She knows the household well. She designs and makes all of our linens. My household is famous for its linens. You must learn how to run a household. You'll have your own to supervise someday."

I felt a slight chill. Maybe she means to marry me off sooner rather than later. Angry, I fingered a small mirror of Zia Terentia's. As she reached for it, I dropped it. Jagged pieces lay at her feet.

"Clumsy girl!" she snapped. "Don't touch anything of mine again!" She took a deep breath. "Now . . . where was I? Oh, yes . . . the supervision of a household. You must learn to choose things of quality and good taste. I would be embarrassed if any young woman under my influence would do otherwise." In between sentences, she continued to drink until her glass was empty. "Of course, I have sons, but I suppose I will have to train their wives, too. One never knows. . . even with good blood lines." She added with a large burp, "Now run along, and don't bother the servants." At this, I was dismissed. I knew I was to stay out of Zia Terentia's sight. I was relieved that Weaver was there to take me away – and curious how she and I would get along. I followed her to the slaves' compound. In a second floor room, there were large looms, a table, a long bench, two spinning wheels, stools, and several shelves with spindles of brightly colored thread. One loom held white material with a black Greek Key design along the edge. Two swarthy slave women deftly moved shuttles back and forth at other looms. Weaver looked at me. "Now. . . what do you want to do?"

I wanted to leave a mouse in my aunt's bed, but – even more – I really wanted to go back to Arretium. I said, "I want to go home."

Christmas Presence

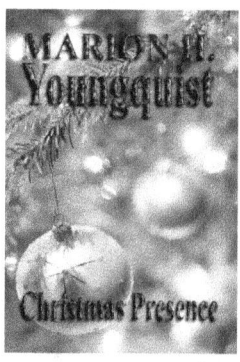

Over five decades, the poet has written an annual Christmas poem. Now, these are all together--available for programs or private devotions during the Yuletide season. Many of my poems focus on characters in the Christmas drama. I wrote them without any order. John Ciardi, a fine poet, commented that a poet must write a hundred poems before a good one is possible. I only hope one or two of these are worthy of the Christmas event. ISBN-13: 978-0977053353 Pages: 62 Type: US Trade Paper Trim Size: 9" x 6" Language: English

Maple Tree Tales

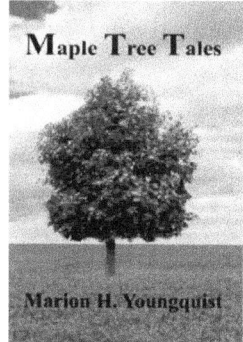

In the fictional town of Whittimore, a historic Sugar Maple stands in Pioneer Park. and observes the constant changes among townspeople--characters in intertwined short stories of difficulty, desire, and destiny--an easy, but an intriguing novel of Americana. Many people are uncertain troubled souls who have difficulty living full and complete lives. Some are like rocks skipped across a pond. Before a rock sinks, tiny circles mark each hit. The water flows on, but a leaf may be trapped, spinning in a whirlpool. Or a small stick is pushed into the other current. Each one seems powerless to change direction. So it seems with people. ISBN-13: 978-0977053339 Pages: 129 Type: US Trade Paper Trim Size: 9" x 6" Language: English

The Rocky Road Year

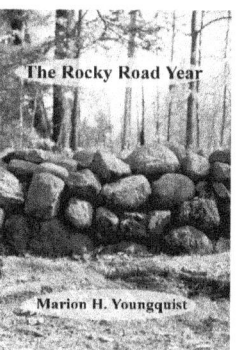

This contemporary novel revolves around Cal, a corporation executive, his wife Tara, and their daughter Anne. When Cal leaves Tara, she goes through the five stages of grief. Their daughter Anne refuses to accept her parents' separation. A Guatemalan missionary trip reunites the three where they are changed in unexpected ways--each with a new future. Their story provides insight into American family life, affected by the business world. This is a good novel for discussion by book clubs. Marion Youngquist's THE ROCKY ROAD YEAR relates the trials and upsets of a middle-aged woman's rocky year after her husband of many years ups and leaves her. The reader can relate to Tara's feelings of loss, confusion and betrayal as she watches the man she has loved and nurtured through many years of marriage, the birth and bringing up of a lovely daughter, and playing the role of helper as he moves up the ladder of success in his career although this has involved a myriad of moves from one state to another. ISBN-13: 978-1448637546 Pages: 382 Type: US Trade Paper Trim Size: 9" x 6" Language: English

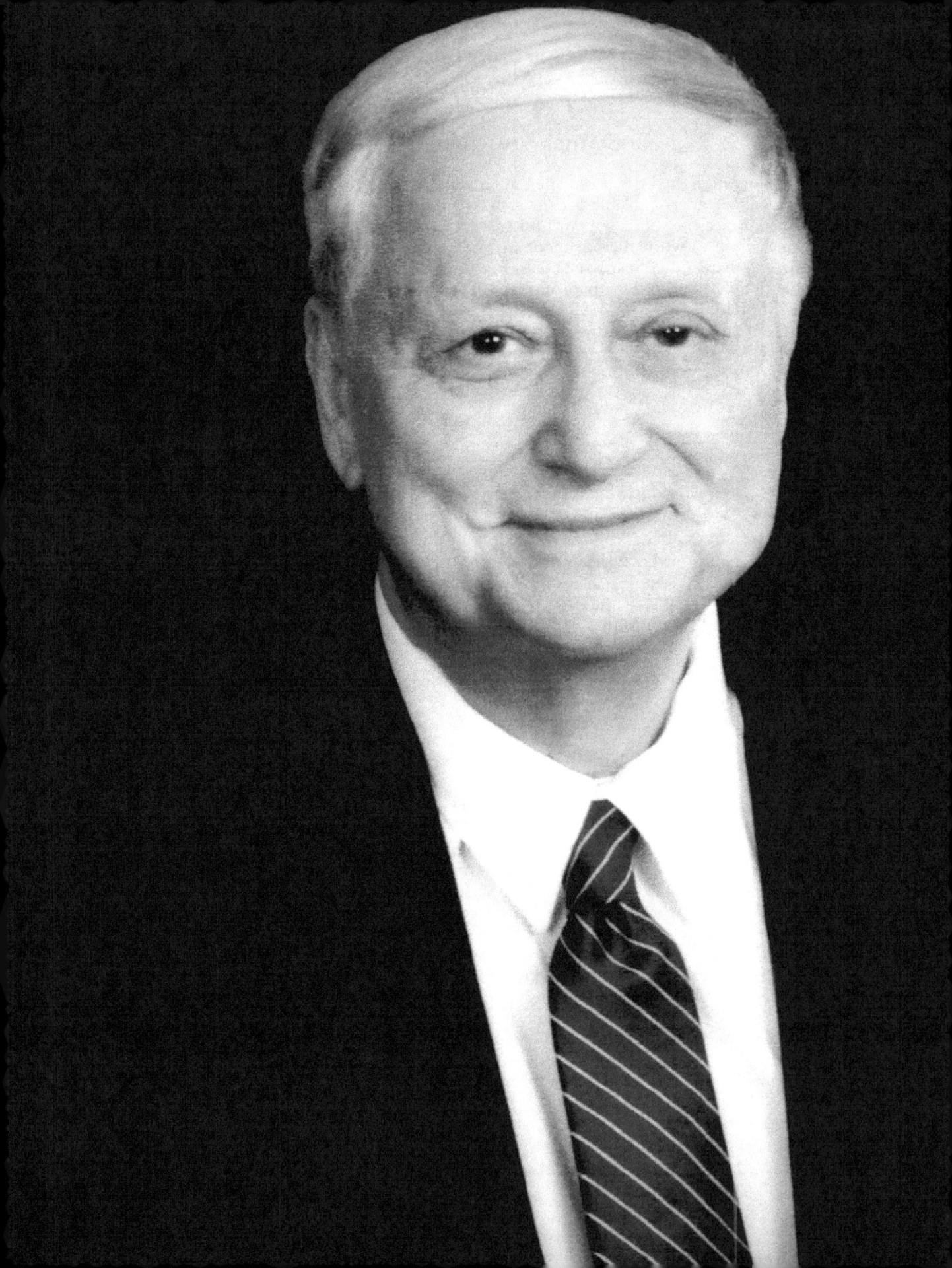

Richard E. Zwez

was born of German, English, and Spanish Peninsular descent in Tela, Honduras, where he attended the American Schools of the United Fruit Company. He has a B.A. from the University of New Orleans where he was in the English Advanced Composition course, has an M.A. from Tulane University, and a Ph.D. in Romance Languages Philology from L.S.U. He taught forty-five years from the elementary through the university levels while teaching Special Education, Spanish, and French in several American cities. He first became known as "Doc" while serving in the Army as a medic while stationed outside of Fairbanks, Alaska, for eighteen months including two winters. He was also stationed at the historic Quadrangle at Fort Sam Houston in San Antonio, Texas.

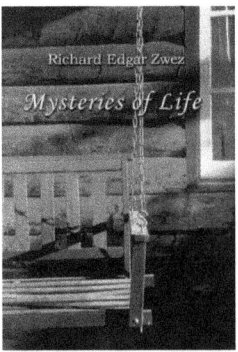

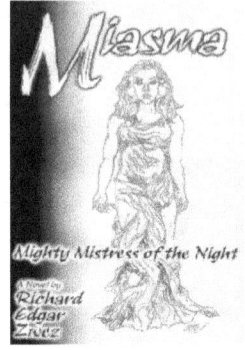

Mysteries of Life

Life is mysterious. When sex, power, ambition, restless imagination fueled by learning, and even supernatural intervention come together a powerful mix is created. When this volatile concoction appears in life its ultimate results can be unpredictable. The explosion can be delayed but not forever. Therefore, we are in a race against time in the mad scramble to bring some sense out of the turmoil while the opportunity still exists. But it can be exciting, not to mention funny, as ridiculous clashes occur. Each one of us has to try to solve the mysteries of life as they come along in our journey through the years since there is always that golden city of peace and happiness beckoning to us from the edge of the horizon. ISBN-13: 978-1494741372 Pages: 194 Type: US Trade Paper Trim Size: 8" x 5" Language: English

Miasma

Miasma is a powerful female archetype. She is a descendant of the goddess Diana. Miasma has immense powers and incomparable physical beauty. She is the exhalation of the soil. As such, she is the guardian of the natural habitat and can harness the tremendous powers of nature to do her bidding. In the novel, she fights with all of her fabulous strength the evildoers who try to enrich themselves at the expense of their fellow men. Throughout the novel, she develops more and into a caring, beautiful, alluring being whose silvery majesty adds to the splendor of the night. She shows that she is capable of loving and falling in love. As a fabulous being, she adds to the lore of Louisiana where tales of the supernatural have always been fascinating. The novel is filled with action, adventure, mystery, splendor, and thrills but also is a work of literary merit. ISBN-13: 978-0759623903 Pages: 196 Type: US Trade Paper Trim Size: 8" x 5" Language: English

Excerpt from Mysteries of Life

"What!"

"They had a long-time affair. Wally."

"Don't kill me with those news!"

"You men are the ones that kill me. You're so busy running your sexual fantasies through your heads with their B-movie level scripts that you're unable to detect the honest to-goodness torrid, real-life liaisons that are happening right under your noses."

"I'm not a bit surprised. After all you're the ones that watch the soap operas. So you're kind to be clued in. Besides, women throughout the eons have competed with each other. So you have developed a sixth sense about it."

"Still, I can't believe that men, generally are so often caught unawares concerning the stirring situations of the heart."

"I guess we're as thick as lead in that department. Most men don't have a clue until the roof of their home comes crashing down on them, and then they are out on the street."

"I know that you're a good friend of Rod's. So I can see how the news of him being deceived would shock you."

"That's not the half of it. How could Keedstick have been so lucky and so long?"

"Lucky how."

"Well, let me tell you. She had all a man would want and plenty of it. She was quite a dish. And that dish was not kept in the refrigerator to cool off."

"The little mind is alert again, eh?"

"I can't help if Nature made me like I am, Martha."

"Yeah, blame Nature, Wally!"

"We're flesh and it sort of tingles sometimes."

"Poor Nature. So many deceptions are committed in your name. Sure. We blame

Nature and everything is cool and copacetic."

"Bull!"

"If that's not the reason, it must be all the money and time you spend making yourselves so alluring and devastating."

"Women want to look nice. Isn't it all right for women to look their best in your book?"

"Best? The men are the ones ending up being bested."

"Beastly is the word."

. . .

. . . "Like they say, It's not the size of the dog in the fight'."

"Exactly my thoughts. We're not large, but we have a lot of fight in us. Put it another way, we'll do what it takes to get to solve a case. The more challenging the case the greater our interest to get to the bottom of it. Even if that bottom is hideous beyond imagining."   "What men's killing instinct won't do when it's not held in check by civilized behavior!"

"The more civilization progresses the more science discovers. Men, if perverted, can use scientific knowledge to wipe out humanity itself. We've seen examples of man's brutal egotism over and over again. But in no case can evil doers rest if they know that justice although slow and patient will get them sooner or later."   "I'm sorry if I was skeptical when you first walked in."

"Your attitude is not surprising,. People have come to equate bigness with quality and efficiency. It is interesting that in these days of mega-hotel chains and gigantic hi-rise hotels, the bed and breakfast people seem to be thriving."

"I'm glad there is room for everyone. Just to let you know that I'm on your wave length of thinking, let me tell you that when my father could not support us, my mother took in boarders to make ends meet."

"That's wonderful."

"Detective Koldak, I also want to thank you for the trust you've given me by allowing me to move about without fearing that I would take advantage of my mobility and decide to skip town."

RICHARD E. ZWEZ

Lazarillos Raros

Lazarillos raros (anthology and commentary of rare books). ISBN-13: 978-1494740900 Pages: 192 Type: US Trade Paper Trim Size: 8" x 5" Language: Spanish

LAZARILLOS RAROS

Lazarillo de Badalona Estudio y Analisis

Lazarillo de Badalona Estudio y Analisis (literary study book). ISBN-13: 978-1494740771 Pages: 146 Type: US Trade Paper Trim Size: 8" x 5" Language: Spanish

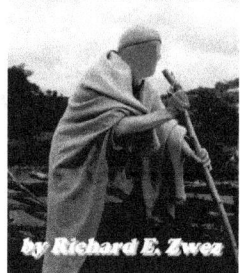

He was also stationed at the historic Quadrangle at Fort Sam Houston in San Antonio, Texas. He later joined the Naval Reserve and served in supply. He's now retired from the Armed Forces. He presided numerous times over the Naval Enlisted Reserve Association, the Fleet Reserve Association, and the Navy Club. He was elected twice commander of the American Legion Post 38. For the Lions he founded the Baton Rouge Metropolitan, Southeast, and South Baton Lions, Clubs and was charter president of the latter two, for these club additions he received three International Extension Awards. He has also done significant service for the Rotary, the Shriners, and the Salvation Army. And he's also been active in various church organizations. He has published literary studies, poems, novellas, and novels dealing with science fiction, mystery, romance, military experiences, teaching situations, the environment, Louisiana life, and repeatedly displayed New Orleans people and the wonderful culture of the Big Easy--always with a preference for the funny side of life. As such he has explored the various facets of humor in the various genres.

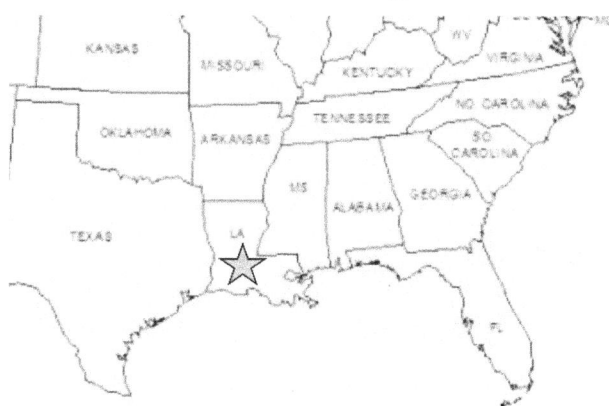

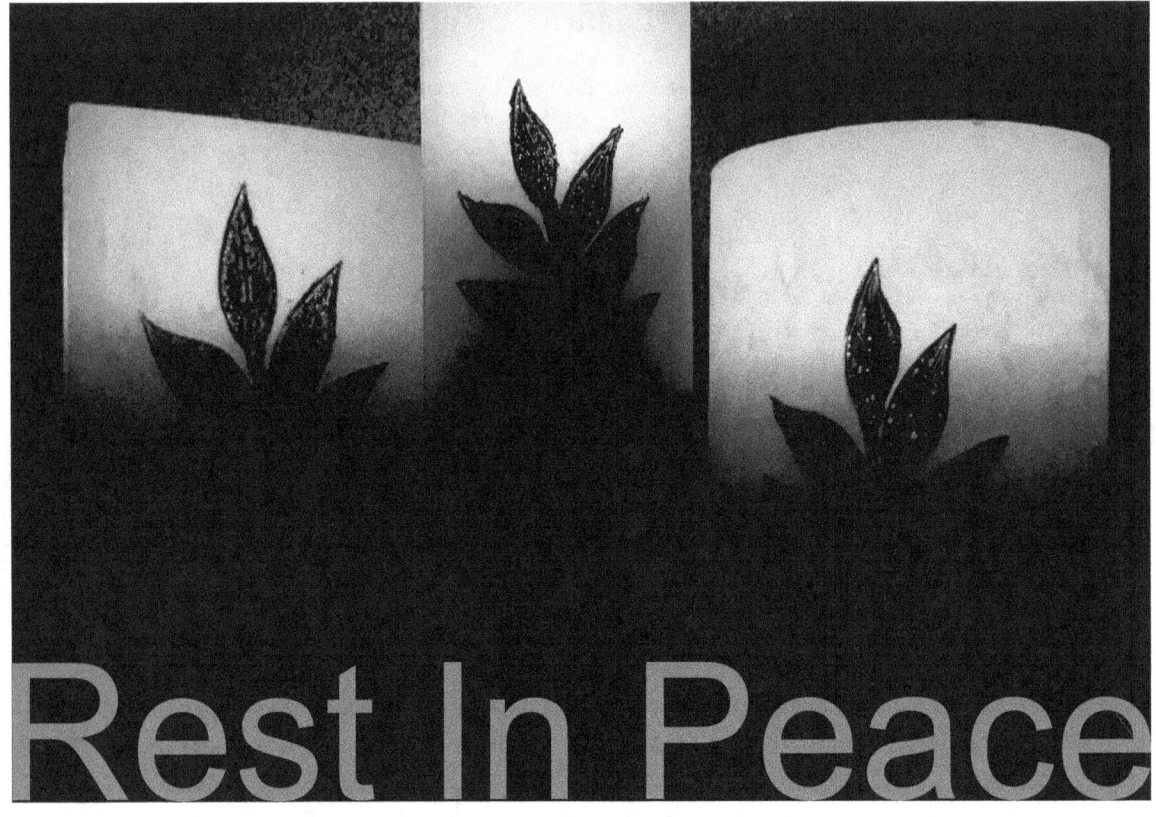

Eternal Candles

Remember loves ones that have returned home. Daily prayers encouraged for everyone mentioned. Memorializes your loved one's name here. Names listed in **BOLD** text are specialized remembrances. Military person name will be highlighted in **RED**, those with purple hearts are in bold purple text. Gifts are tax delectable under 508 (c) (1) (A). Gary Drury Ministries ©™

Back, Barbara — May 10, 2019

Bell, Mary Sylvia — April 12, 2006

Bickett, Anthony — March 01, 2013

Drury, Helen — Sept. 13, 1979

Drury, Julie — Dec. 07, 1995

Drury, Robert B. — August 31, 2015

Drury-Shofner, Priscilla A. — June 24, 2005

Drury Sr., Michael C. — Jan. 23, 1946

Edwards Sr., Bernard — April 30, 2017

Garrett, Danny P. — March 05, 2011

Lamkin, A. Catherine — April 22, 2001

Pendygraft, George Ray — June 08, 1966

Pendygraft, Ruby M. — Oct. 26, 2002

Pendygraft, William C. — Dec.12, 2017

Pendygraft Sr., William R. — Jan. 04, 2002

Scarcelli, Giovanna O. — December 20, 1986

Scarcelli-Lacaria, Mary — August 08, 1982

Scarcelli, Salvatore — March 11, 1985

Shofner, Donald W. — Oct. 31, 1978

Shofner, Oscar — March 12, 1964

Shofner, Patrick — August 17, 2010

Your Loved One's Name can appear here?

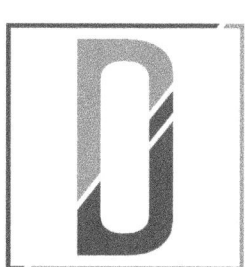

GARY DRURY PUBLISHER | KENTUCKY

www.druryspublishing.com

www.ingramcontent.com/pod-product-compliance
Lightning Source LLC
Chambersburg PA
CBHW081451220526
45466CB00008B/2589